christmas 2000
To Ron   all my love

More Memories

of

Chesterfield

Edited by G.W. Martin

The publishers would like to thank the following companies for their
support in the production of this book

Main Sponsor
Dapet Textiles

Bothams Mitchell Slaney

Chesterfield & District Co-operative Society Limited

Clay Cross Building Society

Fredericks of Chesterfield

Sixt Kenning

C & J Holland Transport Limited

C E Hudson & Son Limited

P R Marriott Drilling

Mount St Mary's College

North Derbyshire Tertiary College

Ruttle Plant

Frank Smith

Tomlinson & White (Contracts) Limited

First published in Great Britain by True North Books Limited
England HX5 9AE

ISBN 1 903204 28 3

Text, design and origination by True North Books Limited
Printed and bound by The Amadeus Press Limited

Introduction

Visitors to Chesterfield town centre are often struck by the many olde-worlde street names which immediately conjure up picturesque links with the past. We can imagine the medieval tradesmen busy in Knifesmithgate and Potters Row. A Shambles denoted the area of a town where the abattoirs were. A gleeman - or gluman, as in Glumangate - was a minstrel. Packers Row was where packhorses started and ended their journeys, while the terminus for packhorses carrying salt from Cheshire was in Saltergate.

In fact the settlement that was to grow into the town of Chesterfield is believed to have originated during the Roman occupation, when the road to the north was being built. For a long time it remained a minor settlement. In the Domesday Book, *Cestrefeld* is described as one of six berewicks to the Royal Manor of Newbold. Thereafter it continued to change hands, belonging at various times to the Crown and to a succession of leading families, and it seems to have grown steadily in size and importance. It acquired a church - always an indication that a place is truly 'on the map.' The architecture of the Parish Church of

St Mary and All Saints is interesting, with features dating from the 13th, 14th and 15th centuries. The font dates from Saxon times, and spent a considerable period buried in the vicarage garden before being dug up again in 1898. Another significant step in the town's development was its Market Charter. King John granted this right in 1204, at the same time making Chesterfield a free Borough, a status confirmed by subsequent charters issued by Elizabeth I and Charles II. In practice the question of self-government seems to have remained something of a moot point for quite some time. Certainly the 6th Earl of Shrewsbury, who was Lord of the Manor during the second half of the 16th century, took the view that his own bailiffs, and not the townspeople, should by rights be in charge of the town. This particular Earl was a colourful figure; he was married to Bess of Hardwick, famous for outliving so many illustrious husbands, and he was also put in charge of the captive Mary Queen of Scots.

Another intriguing part of Chesterfield's history came about in 1688, by which time James II had succeeded Charles II. The story of how the Earl of Devonshire, Lord Danby and John D'Arcy met in the village of

Whittington to conspire against the king, putting James's son-in-law William of Orange on the throne in his place, will be well known to most readers, and Revolution House has been turned into an excellent visitors' attraction.

Shortly after the Glorious Revolution, a wealthy lady named Celia Fiennes, who travelled all over the country around the end of the 17th century and kept a written record of her experiences, came to Chesterfield. She was favourably impressed by the place, and her comments are interesting. She observed that there were coal pits all around and close to town, and the town itself was built of stone. "The town looks weel, the Streets good and the Market very large," she wrote. In fact she seemed particularly taken with the market, where she bought herself "2 very good fatt white pullets for 6 pence both, and I am sure they were as large and as good as would have cost 18

pence if not 2 shillings apiece in London". She also appreciated the beer, commenting that "in this town is the best ale in the kingdom generally esteem'd."

Besides the market, brewing industry and coal mines, it is known that the forge at Staveley was operating at this time, as records have been found there dating back to 1690. However, it was not until the mid-19th century that industry at Chesterfield really began to develop. This was prompted in part by the coming of the railway, and with it George Stephenson. Stephenson arrived in Chesterfield in 1837 to supervise the construction of the Midland line from Derby through the town and out to the north. He was already a well-known figure, not least on account of his revolutionary locomotive Rocket, launched eight years earlier and capable of reaching 30 mph. Chesterfield became the famous engineer's home; he married the daughter of a local farmer and took up residence at

Knifesmithgate looking towards Stephenson Place in the mid 1950s

Tapton House, where he died in August 1848. He also invested heavily in local industries. No doubt he became aware, during the course of his railway engineering works, of the wealth of minerals which were to be found in the area, and he set about exploiting this. He was responsible for opening a number of pits and in 1837 was one of the founders of the Clay Cross Company.

Other important industries which were established around this time included the Robinsons family business empire and the Brampton Brewery, which was certainly brewing by 1839; there were also tanneries, potteries and other factories scattered around the town, and the area was becoming increasingly built up. The next hundred years or so saw a dramatic rise in the population of Chesterfield, from 5,000 in the mid-19th century to almost 70,000 in the mid-20th. By the end of the 19th century a new Market Hall had been constructed.

As the 20th century progressed, the industrial pattern began to alter somewhat. The local brewing industry, which had so impressed Celia Fiennes, fell upon hard times: the Chesterfield Brewery was taken over and closed by Mansfield Breweries in 1935, and the Brampton Brewery ceased brewing following its takeover by Warwick & Richardson of Newark in 1951. Other major businesses were established in the area, including the Tube Works and Trebor, the sweet manufacturers who took over the Chesterfield Brewery's old site in Tapton Road. The days of the mines were numbered; everyday life in Chesterfield, as in the rest of Britain, was responding to the motor car and other techno-logical advances - and the scene was set for many of the changes which you will find depicted and described in more detail in the pages of this book.

Contents

Page 7

Street scenes

•

Page 22

Playtime

•

Page 30

Memorable moments

•

Page 41

Nostalgia in colour

•

Page 49

Time in motion

•

Page 58

At the shops

•

Page 65

Making a living

Street scenes

Here we see Knifesmithgate at its junction with Packers Row in the early 1950s; it is interesting to see the old street lamp suspended on a cable above the road. The arches on the right lead to what used to be the cinema and entertainments complex but which in more modern times became the Victoria shopping centre. Credlands Paints, whose large sign dominates one of the buildings on the left, vanished many years ago, and the premises became a heel bar and key cutting shop instead. However, The Baby Linen Shop remained there throughout the second half of the 20th century and is still there at the time of writing.

The tall building on the left is Swallows, Chesterfield's popular department store, which was actually taken over by the Macoward Group of Departmental Stores in 1959. The business is thought to have been started by John Kinder Swallow in the Beehive on Burlington Street, and was certainly trading by 1862; by 1899 it had moved to the corner of Burlington Street and Packers Row. Down the generations, everybody in Chesterfield shopped there, and one of the store's mottos used to be 'Meet your friends at Swallows'. The closure of the store was a loss to the town. Its premises were replaced by a modern building around 1972.

This 1930s view of Knifesmithgate is instantly recognisable, with Victoria Buildings on the left and Swallows on the right. Both these establishments were thriving at the time. Victoria Entertainments Ltd completed a major refurbishment of the premises in 1930, which included the provision of a new café, and the erection of the Cinema - Café - Billiards sign which dominated the frontage for many years. And in 1935, following a serious fire, Swallows opened a new basement selling garden requisites, sports equipment and general ironmongery. The latter category included a top-of-the range, enamelled Acme cabinet wringer-mangle, priced at 85/- and described as 'the perfect piece of kitchen furniture'.

Putting the sheets through the mangle, in the days before spin-dryers, was a tiring job, and you also had to make sure that the children kept their limbs well out of the way when the mangle was being used; little fingers could easily be crushed, and sometimes more serious accidents occurred. Looking through Swallows' 1935 advertisements, we also spotted the following offer which we feel would have been unlikely to get people queuing at the door in later years: Men's corduroy trousers, brown and drab - 10/6. The word 'drab' has, of course, changed its meaning. Whilst in modern times it has come to mean dull and colourless, it used to be the name of a particular type of thick, strong, grey cloth - so a 'drab' suit was actually something to be proud of.

Below: This charming photograph was taken in the 1940s from outside the old Co-op, looking east along Knifesmithgate, past Victoria Buildings, to the building on the corner of Elder Way that used to be Barclays Bank. The face of banking has changed a good deal since then. For perhaps the first three-quarters of the 20th century, people used to set great store by knowing their bank manager personally. Loans, overdrafts, investments and other transactions were discussed and arranged face-to-face in his office, which was often wood-panelled and smelt of pipe-smoke. An appointment would be arranged in advance, you would arrive smartly dressed and perhaps a little nervous, and the meeting would begin with polite enquiries after each other's families before moving on to financial matters, and concluding with advice and a decision stemming from his past knowledge of your affairs and your good character. As the century drew to a close, banking became increasingly automated and impersonal, with computers providing a detailed analysis of your banking history at the touch of a button, holes-in-the-wall to dispense your cash, instant decisions on loans apparently based upon which boxes you ticked on the application form, and telephone and Internet facilities which allow you to set up transactions from your front room at any hour of the day or night (unless the system happens to have gone down) - and by and large, the old days when people stood in awe of their bank manager were gone.

This very clear aerial photograph was taken from the tower of the Parish Church in August 1951. We can look along Knifesmithgate as far as the Town Hall, and down High Street to Market Place and beyond, picking out familiar landmarks such as the Beehive, Woodheads, Dents the chemist, and of course the Market Hall itself. Close examination reveals the latter to be decked out with flags and bunting, which we surmise was due to the Festival of Britain. A hundred years after the Great Exhibition of 1851, the Festival of Britain did a great deal to lift post-war gloom. World War II had been costly in terms of human lives and damage to the economy. The Festival of Britain was a way of boosting the nation's confidence in itself and its

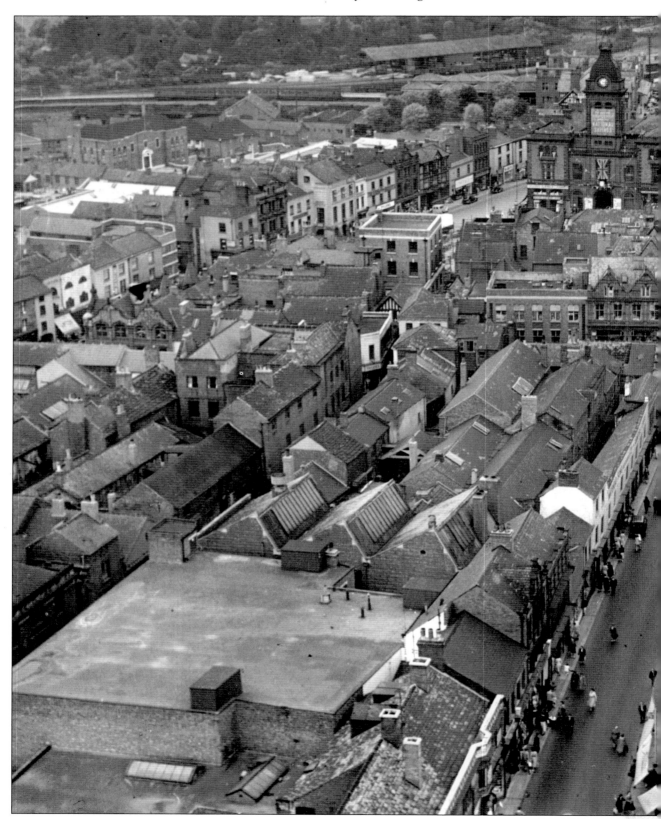

achievements, and building up a mood of optimism. The official Festival, focused around London's South Bank, attracted visitors from all over the world, while towns and cities staged their own events and festivities. Chesterfield's Festival of Britain programme ran from May to September and included exhibitions, agriculture and horticulture shows, concerts, sports, processions, film shows, galas, a circus and a Festival Shopping Week. The Corporation undertook to erect a War Memorial and lay out new gardens behind the Town Hall as permanent mementoes of the Festival, and they also decided to convert the streetlighting from gas to electricity, so that the town could be illuminated as never before.

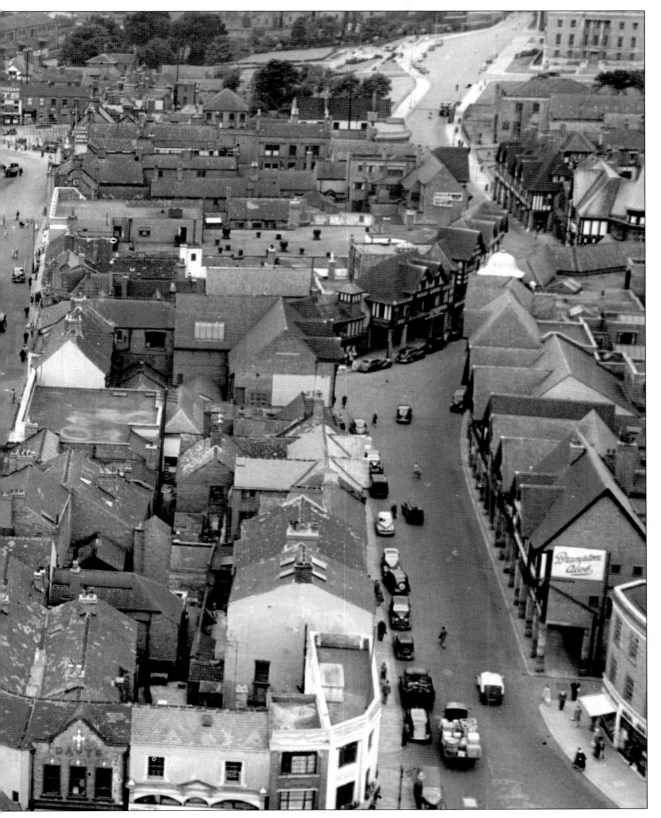

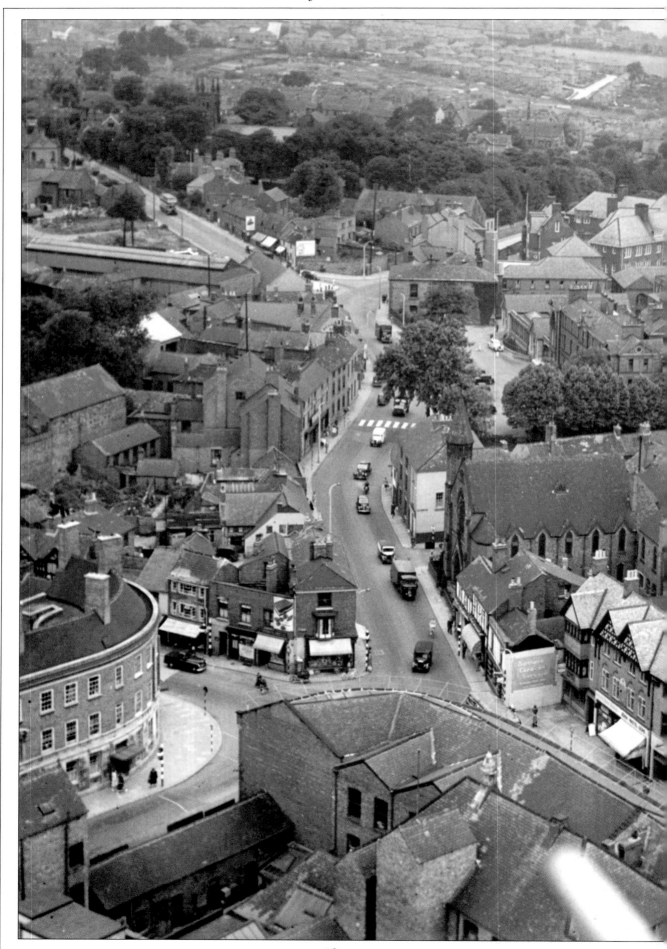

Left: This was the view that would have greeted you if you had climbed up to the top of the Parish Church tower in the summer of '51, and looked out over Chesterfield to the north. A small but significant detail is the large advertisement on the hoarding in the foreground, for Northern Caravan Service. As more families acquired cars, they discovered a whole new range of leisure opportunities: day trips, out-of-town shopping expeditions - and caravanning. Caravan construction became a growing industry, centred mainly in the Humberside area. The early caravans were made from hardboard, but during the 1950s the manufacturers began to use aluminium, which was at that time a relatively new material. The caravan industry went on to promote itself widely, and readers may remember seeing early television advertisements, especially around Bank Holiday periods, inviting viewers to visit the big caravan centres. Anyone who did take up caravanning during those early days will have wry recollections of how basic the 'vans and the sites used to be, in comparison with the luxurious facilities and accessories, including state-of-the-art awnings, which modern caravanners enjoy. But in spite of the lack of home comforts, caravans did offer adventurous families a novel and relatively inexpensive method of getting away for holidays which they might not otherwise have had. It is likely that Northern Caravan Service were already getting a good many interested enquiries by August 1951.

Above: The sign outside says 'Electrical Warehouse', but many readers will have fond memories of this building as the Durham Ox. Caught by the camera in 1963 in the process of demolition, this old pub on Chatsworth Road had stopped serving drinks some few years earlier, and had in fact spent its last years as an electrical salesroom. On the side wall of the Durham Ox we can still see the shape of the building which used to stand next to it, but which has already been pulled down. Demolition is well under way on the building to the right, too, with just a few heaps of bricks still standing to show where the walls used to be. After the site was cleared, a petrol station and shop were built here. The early 1960s were a bad time for historic inns; another of Chesterfield's very old pubs, the Half Moon Inn, also closed at about the same time, but up to the time of writing the premises have remained occupied.

Above: Tailors and shoe shops abound in this snapshot of Burlington Street in the 1940s, though the purchase of a new pair of shoes and new items of clothing would have required much careful thought before parting with those precious ration coupons. However, Burtons, whose distinctive lettering can be seen on the left in the middle distance, was flourishing around this time. Other value-for-money menswear shops during the first half of the 20th century included the popular Weaver to Wearer chain and The Fifty Shilling Tailor, or FST, who used to be at 16 Burlington Street and who, true to their name, used to sell suits for just fifty bob. Almost off our picture to the right, near the camera, is the old Burlington Street branch of Boots. Generations of shoppers have looked upon Boots as much more than a chemist. By the end of the 20th century, large Boots branches offered a good selection of gifts and fancy goods as well as toiletries and medicaments. During the 1940s it had different strings to its bow: around that time the shop advertised itself as 'the farmers' chemist', and its advertisements elected to highlight such items as sheep medicines, pig powders, cereal seed dressing, and Udsal, a soothing ointment for cows' teats.

Above right: Chesterfield Town Hall was built in the years leading up to the second world war. The foundation stone was laid by the Mayor, Cr H P Short, on 15th April 1936, and the opening ceremony was performed by Her Grace the Duchess of Devonshire almost exactly two years later, on 6th April 1938. The initial plans and preparations for the new civic centre had begun many years previously, and the first major step was taken in 1930, when the Corporation purchased the nine-acre Rose Hill Estate. Architects were then commissioned to plan a civic centre for the town. Important factors were that it should have road access, and that it should be 'convenient and harmonious'. All these criteria were met. The harmonious appearance of the building was achieved by using Portland stone facing on the lower storeys and dressings, which contrasts nicely with the warm brick tones of the upper portion. The fine triple-arched portico and pediment in the centre of the long south-facing front give the hall great dignity. Road access took the form of a new road from Knifesmithgate to Clarence Road, and new streets running down the sides of the building from Saltergate. The original plans also made provision for steps and a pedestrian approach from West Bars, but these features were not added until the late 1980s. Our photograph was taken in 1959, from the Market Hall.

Below: This bird's-eye view of Chesterfield in 1951 was taken from the Parish Church tower, looking south along St Mary's Gate towards Lordsmill Street; Beetwell Street is off to the right, with Hipper Street branching off to join Markham Road. At that time, the north-south route took traffic heading north on the A61 straight up Lordsmill Street, St Mary's Gate and Holywell Street. This clearly became a problem as the volume of traffic increased. Statistics reveal that whereas in 1953 only one adult in every twenty-four, nationwide, owned a car, this had increased to one adult in seven a decade later, and the trend continued. Add to this the growth in the population of Chesterfield, which in 1951 stood at just 70,000, and it is plain to see why eventually the town's road network would need to be adapted. Through traffic had to be diverted around the town; the movement of motorists in the town centre had to be controlled; and there had to be somewhere for them to park when they got there. Changes on the southern approaches included a new roundabout at the junction of Lordsmill Street and Markham Road, and various new stretches of dual carriageway. A new shops and offices complex erected just off the roundabout at Markham Road became the home of the Inland Revenue and the Social Security offices. Beetwell Street became wider and straighter and was chosen as the location for the new police station.

Bottom: Some of the businesses which we can see on this 1952 view of Knifesmithgate were familiar to generations of Chesterfield shoppers. On the left is Greaves' furniture shop; many a married couple set up house with furniture from T Greaves & Co, as their parents had done before them. We tend to associate hire purchase with the post-war years and the growth of the consumer culture, and certainly buying things on credit became more common then, especially when people began to acquire cars, fridges and other expensive household appliances. However, it was possible to buy on the never-never long before that. It

is said that Rolls, an early manufacturer of twin-tub washing machines, was one of the first companies to offer payment by instalment as an inducement to buy their products. Certainly in the years between the wars, Greaves were offering bedroom suites at prices ranging from ten guineas (£10-10s-0d) to sixty guineas (£63-0s-0d), or, alternatively, at half-a-crown (2/6d) per week. However, advertisements from that era which offer easy payment schemes seem pleasantly low-key when compared to the more forceful advertising to which we were subjected by the end of the 20th century, bombarding us with all manner of 0 per cent finance, cash-back, buy-now-pay-later deals to tempt us to into spending more than we can really afford.

We believe this view of Knifesmithgate dates from the early 1960s. More than 50 years of tradition came to an end in 1965 when the last film was shown in the Victoria. Landmarks in the history of this particular cinema include a number of name changes, refurbishments and changes of ownership. Known in its early days as the Brydon Picture Palace, it subsequently became the Victoria Picture House, and, much later, the Gaumont. Extensions to the Victoria Hall in the early 1920s resulted in a completely new auditorium which was opened in December 1924. More refurbishments later in the same decade converted the cinema to show talkies, and the first

film to be shown when it re-opened was the great Warner Bros film The Singing Fool, of which the highlight for many people was Al Jolson's tremendous rendition of the song 'Sonny Boy'. Rebuilding continued at the Victoria, to create a new shops complex with café and ballroom, and upon completion the facade bore the Cinema - Café -

Billiards legend which can be seen on several of our photographs. In 1956 the property was sold by Victoria Entertainments Limited to the Rank Organisation. After the closure of the cinema in 1965, it became a bingo club for a time. More recently another major phase of rebuilding was implemented, to create the Victoria Shopping Centre.

Bottom: Knifesmithgate, with Elder Way leading off to the right, is seen here in 1950. The only significant structural alterations along this stretch since that time have been to the frontage of the building to the left of the Co-op department store. As we can see, this building in 1950 had round headed entrances. These round arches have since been replaced by a modern frontage. The Co-op remained much the same, and the mock-Tudor exterior of the Victoria Buildings, constructed around the 1920s, has remained largely unaltered, although the interior is very different. When the photograph was taken, the Victoria comprised a cinema, a ballroom with a well-sprung floor, a large restaurant and a billiard room, while leading off from the pavement there were shops behind the columns. In 1957 the cinema operated as part of the Gaumont chain, and in 1965 it closed with the film Tom Jones, starring Albert Finney and Susannah York. By the end of the 20th century, the entertainment sections of the Victoria were a fading memory, and the interior of the building had been transformed into a modern shopping complex, the Victoria Centre. The buildings opposite also look much the same, although again the businesses inside them have changed.

Right: No precise date has been recorded for this photograph. However, we note that the Market Hall is without its dome, which was removed during the 1960s and was absent for many years; and we also note that the Westminster Bank building, seen in the distance to the left, is surrounded by scaffolding,

which may or may not be an indication that demolition is about to take place. By 1970 this building had been pulled down and new premises built on the same spot to accommodate the Westminster Bank. The F-suffix on the registration plate of the Triumph saloon which is heading away from the camera confirms the date as being no earlier than August 1967. The licensing system of using a letter as a suffix to denote the year of manufacture of the vehicle was introduced in the early 1960s, and with it, a whole new national status symbol was created - which was good news for the motor trade. Having your brand-new car delivered and parked on your drive, ready for use on 1st August, was sure to set the neighbours' curtains twitching, and the new generation of car-mad youngsters used to vie with each other to be the first to spot a brand-new vehicle on the road.

about an attractive young lady - who happens to be smoking - only to be advised by his mate to forget it - 'it's like kissing an old ash-tray.' However, by that time the cigarette culture was far too well-established to be changed overnight.

Top: Cavendish Street is seen here in the early 1960s. Heading away from the camera is a Ford Anglia, sometimes affectionately called an Angular because of the sharp angle between roof and rear window and its pointed rear corners. Leisure time could be spent at the ABC Regal, where this week's offering was Sparrows Can't Sing. It would be nice to be able to give this British-made comedy-melodrama

Above: The Vauxhall parked along the east side of Cavendish Street in 1964, which we believe to be an FB Victor Estate, is proudly advertising Rothman's King Size in an era when the public was perhaps just beginning to worry about the connection between cigarettes and lung cancer. A decade or so earlier, smoking had been entirely socially acceptable, even desirable. The notion of banning smoking in public places would have seemed very odd indeed. When evidence to suggest that smoking caused lung cancer was first announced, it came as a real shock to smokers everywhere, and there was great reluctance to accept the scientists' findings. To hammer the message home and discourage smoking, the government began a series of hard-hitting advertising campaigns, backed up with the imposition of stark health warnings on all tobacco advertising. Readers may remember some of the adverts which appeared on television in those days; there was, for instance, a rather poignant scene in a pub, with one youth passing a favourable comment to his mate

from the Elstree studios a glowing write-up, but unfortunately critics of the day found little to praise about it. However, it did feature a young Barbara Windsor, along with Roy Kinnear and Arthur Mullard. Alternatively, you could buy a Hi-Fi unit from Roy Smith and stay at home and listen to records. During the 1960s we got excited about stereophonic sound in much the same way as, several decades later, we enthused about the crystal clear sound quality of digitally-recorded CDs. Getting your first stereo record player was a real thrill. Mono records could still be played on stereo equipment, but new stereo LPs could be damaged by the heavier mono pick-ups and needles. Readers may remember that Decca, who had a number of supergroups including the Rolling Stones on their label, had an ingenious colour-coding system, with a red border around the inner record sleeve for mono recordings, and blue for stereo - so if you took your treasured LPs to parties, you had to try and make sure that they all went back into the right sleeves.

Left: The composition of this photograph, taken in 1962, might almost have been planned as a publicity shot for Halfords: the business describes itself as a Motor, Moped and Cycle Store, and lined up outside we duly have a selection of motor vehicles, a token small motorbike or moped, and a cyclist pedalling along towards Hoyles. Also by the kerb is a motor-cycle and sidecar, or 'combination', as they were called. These used to be popular means of transport, but in subsequent decades they became much less common. Often favoured by young couples, they were an economical and fun way of getting about, but once the little bundles of joy started arriving it was generally accepted that the time had come to trade the combo in - often with great regret - and move up to a family car. Travelling in the sidecar, or 'bubble', was great fun; it was more luxurious than travelling pillion, and, being so low to the ground, it gave the sensation of tremendous speed even when you were actually moving quite slowly. From the driver's point of view they were a little unwieldy and had to be manoeuvred with care, as the combination had to be steered round corners, rather than leaned into them like a solo motorcycle.

Above: Many readers will remember going to the Odeon on Holywell Street; not so many will remember going there when it was still called the Picture House. It was as the Picture House that the cinema first opened in September 1923. Its original frontage was not, however, as impressive as the one seen here. Around that time, a scheme to widen Holywell Street was in progress; this involved major works and was on-going until around 1930. During this same period a considerable amount of alteration, extension and redevelopment was carried out to the cinema frontage. Eventually this resulted in the very fine building which was renamed the Odeon in 1938, and which by the end of the 20th century had become the Winding Wheel conference centre, after standing empty for a number of years following the closure of the cinema in 1981. Our photograph was taken in the 1950s, and the busy zebra crossing reminds us that this was an era when road safety was a matter of growing public concern. The police made a point of holding free road safety demonstrations, often in Queens Park on a bank holiday, to educate people about the causes of road accidents and how to prevent them. But traffic continued to build up, and eventually more drastic measures such as ring roads, one way systems and pedestrian zones had to be introduced to keep cars and people out of each other's way.

Playtime

Above: This splendidly evocative photograph, taken by Mr Martin, has captured the light-and-shade effects of the autumn sunshine as a father takes his family for a walk amongst the fallen leaves in Queens Park in late 1969. Queens Park has pleasant footpaths, a boating lake, and a cricket ground where readers may well have spent sunny afternoons watching Derbyshire; at the time of the photograph, the pitch would still have been regularly used for County cricket. In the years before TV, and even before the wireless, the bandstand was a popular place to go on a Sunday afternoon, and concerts are still sometimes held here during the summer months. Tennis courts, recreational areas and a children's play area continue to provide good amenities for the local people. By the end of the 20th century, youngsters were tending to spend rather more of their leisure time at home than they used to, indulging in indoor amusements such as computer games and a wide choice of TV viewing. However, there are still plenty of us who enjoy being out in the fresh air, and the park, within easy access of the town centre, makes a pleasant place to eat sandwiches in the middle of a working day. An attractive place in its autumn colours, as seen here, Queens Park is equally colourful in springtime with its flowers and blossoms.

From the top of the Town Hall, we are looking down on the War Memorial, seen in the foreground, and our view extends across Shentall Gardens towards West Bars, over the road and into the goods yard of the Market Place station. At the time of the photograph, in 1954, the goods yard was occupied by Arnold Laver and was used as a timber yard. Arnold Laver moved out to Brimington Road in the late 1950s, and an office block for the Accountant General's Department of the Post Office - known as the AGD - was built on the site of the old goods yard. That office block was demolished in 1997, and another Post Office building took its place on the same site. The railway line which we can see was the main line to Skegness. Known as the East Coast Railway, the original intention was that it should go right through to Manchester. In the event it never got any further than Chesterfield, and the line closed in the mid-50s.

Above: Few readers will recognise this picture as Newbold Road, Chain Bar; but this is what this part of the road used to look like in 1954. When you travelled out of the town centre on Newbold Road at this period, once you got past Newbold House the area was all farms, open fields and country roads. There were also a number of collieries in the Newbold Area. The winding gear visible behind the trees here belonged to the pit known as Tin Chimney Mine. This was the last mine in the area to carry on working, but it closed down not long after this photo was taken. Within the space of less than half a century this scene changed almost beyond recognition. Now, of course, it is all built up and the road has been made wider, but the houses at the roadside are still there.

Above right: This pleasant, sleepy little scene was taken in Newbold Village on a sunny day in 1952. Every single building in the photograph has been pulled down, with most of the demolition taking place between 1959 and 1960. The small shop on the right was a greengrocers, trading under the name of Stones. The bicycle leaning against the door with the basket on the front handlebars would be the errand boy's bicycle. Looking along that row, past the wooden railings, we can see that the end building is set back a little. This used to be the Cross Daggers, which was a very old pub. In more recent times all this has changed, the road has been widened and flats have been built on the spot where the Cross Daggers and other buildings once stood.

Right: Newbold Back Lane, photographed here in 1952, was a narrow lane which joined Newbold Road almost opposite Newbold House. From the lone tree at the bottom, footpaths led to Ashgate and the donkey racecourse. To the left, the lane joins Hawksley Avenue, and that end is now a built-up area. The field where the cows are grazing peacefully was cut through in the early 1960s by a wide motor road to Ashgate, and in the valley, beyond the hedge with the three trees, great housing estates now cover the area. By contrast, the end of the lane closer to the camera has not changed much up to the time of writing; it is a little wider, and the hedges are higher. The little chap who is out for a ride on his tricycle is looking across towards Green Farm, off this picture to the right.

Below: This rural scene is actually the outskirts of Newbold, in 1949. The horse and rider are passing Newbold House, which was a large and very old stone-built residence, with extensive outbuildings, stables etc. Between 1904 and 1937 it was the home of Lt-Col and Mrs Orange-Bromehead. It then stood empty for many years from 1938, but was once again occupied for a short time just prior to its demolition in the late 1950s. Flats now stand on this site. Anyone riding a horse along this stretch of road today would be well advised to wear reflective clothing and a hard hat instead of the casual hacking jacket and headscarf which were good enough for road traffic conditions in 1949. Interestingly, at the precise moment when the camera shutter clicked, the horse was in mid-trot with all four hooves off the ground.

Right: The cyclist seems to be finding it hard work, pushing his bicycle up the hill, and this gives a fair indication of the gradient of this stretch of Boythorpe Road. The trees which run alongside the pavement to the right of the road form the boundary of Queens Park Annexe. The photograph was taken in 1958, some three years before the grounds were laid out for sports use. This part of the park then became a popular place for clubs and schools to hold their athletics meetings. Down towards the bottom of the hill on the left, just above the truck, is the Boythorpe Inn. Some of the cottages higher up on the same side were occupied by miners who worked at Boythorpe Colliery, further up the hill. The colliery has now closed, all these cottage have gone, and in their place are pairs of semi-detached houses.

Below: This scene in Queen's Park dates from the late 1960s and shows not a County match, but a local mid-week fixture. By the end of the 20th century only local teams and Derbyshire's Second Eleven played here. However, for 100 years Queen's Park provided one of the most attractive settings for first-class cricket anywhere in the country. When commercial considerations and rationalisation caused the tradition to be broken, giving Derby the monopoly on championship games, it was a sad day for spectators. But some batsmen will have kept less sentimental memories of facing the great seamers of Derbyshire cricket - the likes of Les Jackson, Harold Rhodes, Mike Hendrick and Dominic Cork - on an awkward pitch in Chesterfield's sometimes rather bracing climate. Looking back, we tend to imagine that the sun was always shining in the so-called Golden Age of cricket at the turn of the 20th century, whereas in fact the wind was probably just as cold. Still, there is a certain nostalgic glow around those games of a bygone era, and the ground at Queen's Park has a long and full memory. Here, in 1904, Essex lost to Derbyshire by 9 wickets despite making 597 in their first innings. Derbyshire supporters can look back through the record books and bask in immortal victories such as this - though they may prefer to forget other notable high-scoring matches such as the one against Yorkshire in 1898, when Derbyshire failed to recover from Yorkshire's opening stand of 554 ...

some of the cottages were demolished in the early 1960s. A new inn was constructed, with a car parking area, and this too was named the Goldminers.

Top: In 1970 Chesterfield FC finally put an end to a long run of bad luck and disappointing results and brought the coveted trophy back to Chesterfield. Top contenders for the Division Four Championship that year were Chesterfield, Swansea, Port Vale, Wrexham, Brentford and Aldershot, and by April, with just seven league fixtures left to play, it was clear that Chesterfield was in with a real chance. Four out of their seven remaining games were to be played at Saltergate, including the last meeting of all, which was against

Above: In a coal-mining area, it is perhaps a little unusual for an inn to be called the Goldminers - but we can all dream ... In fact this elegant inn in Littlemoor was built by a certain Robert Silcock, who did much more than just dream about riches. As a young man he went to the States and joined the goldrush. He struck gold, filed a claim and became very wealthy. Returning to his birthplace a rich man, he built the Goldminers around the middle of the 19th century, and he also built a row of cottages which he named California Row. He then went off on his travels again, and had a narrow escape after being shipwrecked on his final voyage home. Having finally satisfied his wanderlust, he settled in Newbold, opened a shop in Bargh's Lane and took an active part in council affairs. He is buried in the churchyard of Newbold Parish Church. Of the buildings which he put up in the village, the inn and

Peterborough. In the event the match itself was a rather one-sided affair, with Chesterfield outclassing Peterborough from start to finish. But for the fans, the excitement lay in savouring every moment as they watched their team take the Championship. At the end of the match, 14,250 Chesterfield supporters gave their team a standing ovation. A civic reception was arranged by the Mayor, Councillor V S Allen, as seen in our photograph. The victory came as a fitting climax to what everybody agreed was easily the team's best season since winning the Third Division Championship in 1936. Outstanding players included skipper John Archer and the mid-field star Tom Fenoughty, who was selected to receive the Derbyshire Times Player of the Year award. And the team's supporters deserve a mention too; their good behaviour during the season had earned a £100 cheque for charity.

Cinema-goers were a dying breed in November 1985, but the ABC was gallantly trying to pull them in with Return to Oz and Mad Max. Nearly half a century earlier, on 12th October 1936, this cinema had been hailed as one of Chesterfield's greatest leisure attractions when it opened, as The Regal, with a Fred Astaire and Ginger Rogers musical, 'Follow The Fleet', which featured a number of famous songs including 'Let's Face the Music and Dance'. It was renamed the ABC in 1950, and fitted out for cinemascope in 1955. However, television was changing the nation's entertainment habits, and cinemas found it increasingly difficult to tempt

people out of their armchairs. By 1960 there were 10.5 million television sets in Britain, and by 1968 there were 19 million. In 1971 the auditorium was made smaller, comprising only the seats in the circle; the former stalls area was partitioned off, with the front stalls area and the former stage closed off as storage space, and a bar installed where the rear stalls used to be. The bar was called the Painted Waggon, but later it became Spires Bar, as seen on this photograph, and as such outlived the cinema. In fact, before it finally closed the cinema enjoyed another brief lease of life as The Regal, run, so we understand, as a private venture. By the end of the 20th century it had become a nightclub.

Memorable moments

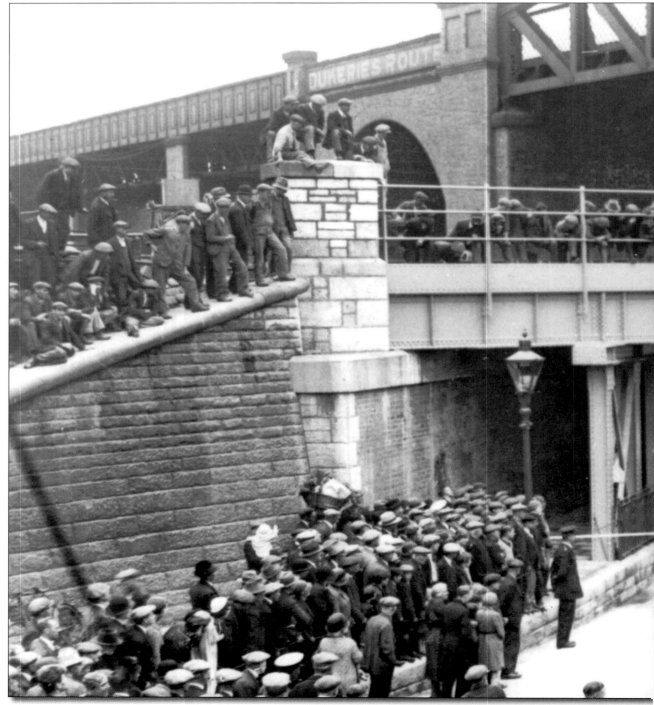

The new Horns Bridge was opened on 24th August, 1932, and was generally considered a thing of great beauty. One of the speakers at the opening ceremony described it as 'one of the most beautiful improvements in the county', and everybody agreed that it added to the amenities of the neighbourhood. Hundreds of people have assembled, as we can see, to witness the cutting of the tape by the Mayor, Alderman T D Sims, JP, who had close connections with the railway. This scheme, as well as replacing the old skew stone bridge built by George Stephenson in 1839, had included the widening of Hasland Road. Over the years, the volumes of both rail and road traffic had increased far beyond what either the bridge or the road had been designed to cope with, leading to growing concern that the narrow road had become a death trap at that point. The total cost of the project was in the region of £30,000. Work on the road widening scheme began in January 1932. When it became necessary to close the bridge to traffic, it was announced that the closure would last for 14 days. This 14-day closure became something of a standing joke locally, as in fact the bridge remained closed for seven weeks. However, the entire project was completed three months ahead of schedule, and Chesterfield was well pleased with its nice wide road and its elegant new bridge.

Above: The month is July 1935, and Corporation Street resounds to the sound of a military band and feet marching in time as the 6th Battalion Sherwood Foresters makes its way to the railway station. Shops along Corporation Street between the wars included Armistead's bicycle shop where you could have bought a Raleigh cycle for £4-19s-6d cash, Millers' furniture shop where sale bargains might have included a Jacobean oak bedroom suite for £8-12s-6d or a four foot solid oak Queen Anne sideboard for £4-17s-6d, and Jays furniture store where budget-priced furniture made in modern factories could be had for less than a pound. As we can see, a few bystanders, out for a Sunday stroll, have stopped to watch the procession pass by, but on the whole the parade seems to have attracted relatively little attention. The 6th Battalion is in fact on a pilgrimage to the Crich Memorial. This pilgrimage, organised by the Old Comrades Association, became an annual event, and was taking place for the 12th time in July 1935. At the ceremony that year, the 6th Battalion was joined by a detachment of the 5th Battalion Sherwood Foresters, along with five Chelsea Pensioners, and wreaths were laid on behalf of other Battalions and numerous branches of the Old Comrades Association. It is likely that many of those present already suspected that the war to end all wars had not in fact done so.

Right: These likely lads and lasses from Johnson Street, Sheepbridge, have been assembled by the photographer on the occasion of the coronation of George VI in 1936. At first glance it might not be crystal clear how they intend to celebrate, but a helpful note on the back of the photograph points out that they are posing in front of Paling's ice-cream float - so we guess they are all going to be treated to some of the delicious ice-cream made by this Unstone firm. Probably these youngsters were too young to understand why the new king was going to be George, and not Edward. Edward VIII had taken the throne upon the death of his father, the popular King George V, in January 1936. Very soon afterwards, rumours about his romantic involvement with Mrs Wallis Simpson began to circulate. A difficult situation developed, which was finally resolved when Edward VIII announced his decision to abdicate rather than give up the woman he loved. So instead of the extrovert, debonair eldest prince that the nation had expected, his shy younger brother, who had intended to follow a career in the Navy, was crowned in his place on the date arranged for the coronation of Edward. George VI made no secret of the fact that he was unprepared for kingship, but he proved an excellent monarch, and his subjects were genuinely saddened by his death from lung cancer in 1952.

Knifesmithgate is positively dripping with flags in this photograph, which we believe to have been taken at the time of King George V's Silver Jubilee in May 1935. The whole nation joined in the celebrations. Chesterfield held a week of Jubilee events, including dances, processions and teas. On Jubilee Day itself, Monday, all the shops were closed and a varied programme of entertainment was put on in the Queen's Park between 2.30 and 10.30 pm. In the evening scores of bonfires were lit all over the region to make a chain of beacons across Derbyshire. There were souvenir mugs and other items to be had; all the schoolchildren were given a Jubilee sixpence, and most schools arranged special lessons

that week to teach pupils about 'the most momentous reign in history.' George V had come to the throne at a difficult time. In 1910, Britain was troubled by industrial unrest and political tensions, and within less than half a decade the country was at war. Around twenty-five years later, unemployment was still at record levels, but national pride was undented, and we hung out the Union Jacks, scraped together what little money we could, and showed our wholehearted support of the monarch. King George made a very moving speech to the nation, concluding by echoing the famous words spoken by Queen Victoria on her Diamond Jubilee, 38 years earlier: 'From my heart I thank my beloved people. May God bless them.'

Above: The Princess Royal is seen here inspecting the ATS Transport section at Queens Park during ATS Campaign Week, September 1941. The ATS was the women's section of the Army. Each section of the armed forces staged regular recruitment drives, and here the ATS, or Auxiliary Territorial Services, is no doubt hoping that their royal visitor will lend a dash of glamour which will attract volunteers - 'Don't Wait,' the poster exhorts. The ATS was not an easy option. The duties of the despatch rider, standing smartly to attention with goggles, gauntlets, mail bag and sergeant's stripes, are self-explanatory; other ATS personnel in the transport section would have been called upon to perform a wide variety of duties covering all aspects of the provision and maintenance of military transport, perhaps including working on tanks which were to be sent overseas. Many ATS recruits had to undergo special training to prepare them for their new duties. They were expected to rapidly pick up the basic principles of engineering and master the necessary practical skills, and once they had completed training and begun their duties, their work would often be physically tiring. And on top of all that, strict military discipline and drilling was required of every section of the armed forces, and the ATS was no exception.

Below centre: By 1976 the Cathedral Vaults, an old inn which used to stand in Market Place, had become structurally unsound. Supporting timbers, properly known as raking shores, were erected to shore the building up until it could be demolished. During the 1950s the Beehive had to be similarly propped up, until the unsafe upper storey had been removed. The Vaults was a Regency building, though its style was more commonly described by local people as 'pretty windows' on account of its fine stained glass windows. Estate agents' boards on the dark brick building adjoining The Vaults still appear to be optimistically inviting enquiries, but at the time this photograph was taken it was a little late for that; both buildings were pulled down very shortly afterwards. The brick building used to belong to the Home & Colonial Stores, a chain of grocery shops which in the early to mid-20th century had a branch in many towns up and down the country. The new structure which was put up in the place of these two properties, and became the offices of a building society, was not altogether dissimilar to the old Vaults.

Below: From the top of the Town Hall, the message blazes clearly into the night sky: Victory! Not that anybody in August 1945 was likely to forget, even for a second, that we had won the war. The date of the photograph is given as 15th August of that year - the day after the Japanese surrender finally marked the end of all hostilities. This anniversary is now commemorated as VJ Day - Victory in Japan; the unconditional surrender of Germany on 7th May is now known as VE Day - Victory in Europe. As far as most people were concerned, once we had defeated Hitler the war was as good as won, and jubilation broke out all over Britain during May. The flags and bunting went up and there were public thanksgiving services, street parties, Victory dances and all manner of celebrations. The sense of relief was tremendous. During the course of World War II, the Allies had dropped a reported 2,700,000 tons of bombs on Germany, and, perhaps surprisingly, official statistics showed that fewer British lives had been lost than during the first world war. But world tensions did not miracu-

lously melt away the moment the Japanese signed the treaty on 14th August 1945. The Cold War lay ahead, with all those very real fears of Reds under the bed and nuclear war just around the corner. The sinister image of the Iron Curtain, which Churchill first spoke of in March 1946, was to remain with us for decades.

Bottom: Britain has won the war, and the good people of Loco Terrace, Hasland, are celebrating as a community, with a party out in the street. Ration coupons will have been pooled and every family will have chipped in with whatever goodies they have managed to get their hands on, for the celebratory meal. Although the war was officially over, things did not return to normal overnight. Men had to wait for their demob papers, rationing remained in force for another nine years, and as the country counted the cost of the war, it became clear that the national economy was in a bad way. And people had to adjust mentally too; women had become used to working and enjoying greater independence than ever before, while the men, when they got back, often had to start looking for work and rebuilding their lives. There were still shortages of all kinds of everyday items, partly because of the need to export as many goods as possible to help the economy. However, items like bananas and proper soft white bread that had disappeared from the shops during the war began to reappear, and ordinary consumer goods gradually came off ration. Sweets came off in 1949, but rationing did not end completely until 3rd July, 1954.

Below: Carlisle Street, Sheepbridge, used to have a wooden Mission at the top of the street, with a portable caravan which sold fish and chips next to it; but here we see Carlisle Street transformed with Union Jacks and a long table spread with a right royal feast for the children of the street to enjoy - just as soon as the tiresome business of saying 'cheese' for the photographer is over! The year is 1936, and the occasion is the coronation of King George VI. On the back of the photograph is a list of names which shows this really was a family occasion: we have Mrs Roderick and three little Rodericks, Mrs Newall and two little Newalls, Mrs Bowler and two little Bowlers, et cetera. Street parties like this one were taking place all over Chesterfield that day, and indeed all over the country; this used to be the tradi-tional way of celebrating events of national importance. In each street, little communities would have been collecting money for months and deciding amongst themselves who would provide what goodies for the party. Often, if funds stretched, there would be a small present for each of the kiddies to take away with them. Few readers are likely have very clear memories of 1936 coronation parties, but more will remember the 1953 coronation celebrations - though unfor-tunately on that occasion it rained rather heavily, and all over town hasty last-minute arrangements were made to hold the parties indoors instead.

Right: Chesterfield's first Hospital Carnival Week took place in September 1929. The objective was to raise money to provide and maintain 30 additional beds, and also to pay for the first year's building work on a new ward. So Chesterfield & District Hospital Demonstration Committee worked in conjunction with various other bodies to stage a full week of fund-raising events. To stimulate the public's interest, a competition was run in the Derbyshire Times, inviting readers to vote for the Carnival Queen; young ladies were invited to send in their photos, from which six were selected to appear in the paper each week for five weeks, and at the end of that period readers were asked to fill in a ballot slip, with a cash prize for the reader who correctly predicted the top six ranking order. Out of all the entrants, whose ages ranged from under ten to late teens, seventeen-year-old Miss Nelli Rixon was selected, and presided over a very successful carnival week. It began with a brilliant carnival procession on the Saturday, and events through the week included dances, community singing, whist drives, motorcycle competitions, a comic fancy-dress football match between the Westminster Bank's team of Pirates and Eyre & Sons' team who called themselves the Chesterfield Armchairs, a number of beauty contests including an ankle compe-tition, and of course the Fancy Dress contest pictured here. Hospital Carnival Week was a great success and went on to become an annual event.

All manner of things have been hawked at Chesterfield Market over the years, and here we see a patent medicine salesman trying his patter on the crowd. It has to be said that they do not look a terribly promising bunch of customers. The lad with the cap on seems to be more interested in whatever he has cupped in his hands; we have a strong suspicion that he has brought his pet mouse with him. The date of this little scene is 1938. Family medicine at that time was still dominated to a large extent by patent recipes for remedies passed down from mother to daughter, and a number of drinks were sold which were supposed to cure all manner of ills.

These mainly contained herbal ingredients - although as often as not the recipe was top secret; these were the days before consumer groups insisted on the right to know what they were buying. Often these patent tonics tasted quite nice - sometimes of liquorice, or sarsaparilla - and probably they did contain things that were good for you. However, this trader seems to be dealing in ointments or potions rather than medicinal drinks, and from his props it seems that he is trying to impress his audience with the wonders of science. Let's hope that he has some good tricks up his sleeve, because so far they are all looking decidedly sceptical.

Nostalgia in colour

This busy market scene was captured during 1963, surely on a Saturday during the summertime. Ayres, whose fruit and veg stall is in the centre of the picture, started up with a barrow in New Square around 1910. We believe that the group of ladies who are approaching the camera, but with their eyes turned towards the fruit stall, have come out of the hair stylist above Maxwells; perhaps they are thinking that a piece of fruit would make a nice refreshing lunch. Maxwells was a popular ladies' dress shop which also had a bridalwear department. The projecting section was one of three Regency arches which stood on the north,

south and east sides of the Market Place. The other two remain in a renovated form, but the one seen here has gone. At the time of our photograph it was occupied by T P Woods wines and spirits merchants, established in 1844. Of all the buildings seen in the background here, only one - the Midland Bank - remains. One of the Midland Bank's claims to fame is that it was the first bank to offer its business customers night safe facilities, so that they could deposit cash outside banking hours. This scheme was introduced in 1938. Further along to the left the NatWest Bank still occupies the same site as did the old Westminster Bank, but in a new building.

Above: There are three things which are particularly striking about photographs of street scenes from the 1950s: the lack of yellow lines along the kerb, the complete absence of plastic carrier bags, and the scarcity of ladies wearing jeans or slacks. This view of Cavendish Street dates from 1959, and flared skirts are much in evidence. Another sign of the times is the pair in uniform who are crossing the road, reminding us of the days when buses had a driver and a conductor. These two will no doubt have just called into Daveys for a sandwich or a roll, and will now be going back to their bus, parked near the crooked spire. All the buildings seen here survived the 20th century, although those on the left all changed hands. Looking straight ahead into Cavendish Street we can see frontage of the old Regal Cinema, with its canopy. The Regal was later taken over by

the Associated British Cinema's ABC chain, before finally closing. The premises later became a club called the Zanzibar. To the right, the stone building was still William Deacons Bank in 1959; it remained a bank, but by the end of the century had became the Royal Bank of Scotland.

Above right: Striding out purposefully across New Square Market in 1956 is the Rev E Gregson, who was at that time vicar of Christ Church, Stonegravels, a post he held for some 15 years. Scenes such as this give some flavour of the tremendous popularity of Chesterfield's open air markets; whatever changes and developments come about in the town centre, open air markets are one thing that simply must stay. The mother and daughter in the foreground have dresses of the same material, which leads us to think it likely that mother has a Singer or a Jones sewing machine at home. Sewing

machines became extremely popular around this time, offering exciting new possibilities to women of all ages. There was a Jones sewing machine centre inside Eyres Furnishing Stores in Holywell Street, which sold not only the machines themselves but dressmaking patterns, buttons and virtually everything the home dressmaker could need. Enterprising young women could follow the latest fashions without breaking the bank, and housewives with growing children no longer had to scrimp and save in order to provide new clothes for their families. For young couples setting up home, sewing machines were invaluable for running up curtains and other soft furnishing coverings. At the same time, the wartime 'make do and mend' philosophy still lingered, and most families had their 'rag bags' where they collected waste material which could then be recycled, very often into imaginative fancy dress costumes for the kiddies.

Below: In the early days after the removal of the market stalls in New Square - pictured here in 1959 - and also in the main Market Square, the space was available for car parking, free of charge! A good selection of late-50s cars has assembled itself on what used to be the pig market, or Swines Green; the name was changed to New Square in the second half of the 19th century. The pale-coloured Ford, which is partially obscured by the group of pedestrians but which we believe to be a Zodiac, is the shape of things to come and contrasts sharply with the dark-coloured 'sit-up-and-beg'-type vehicles that had been prevalent hitherto. Behind the Ford we can see the right-hand part of Dents' shop, which was occupied by 'Sandy' Smart, Dents' optician. Close inspection shows two rectangular windows joined by a connecting 'bridge'. Use a little imagination, and what have we got? Yes - a pair of spectacles! Next to

Dents we can see the old Star & Garter pub. The whole block was demolished in the early 1960s.

Bottom: Many readers will remember the days prior to the 1970s when Holywell Cross, seen here in 1958, was a busy shopping area. When the road layout was changed to create a one-way system around a very large car park, all the buildings seen on this picture to the left of the chapel had to be pulled down. These included the popular green-grocer, Damms, and The Tripe Shop next door. It is highly probable that many younger readers will never have tasted tripe; whilst it cannot be said that tripe is in itself an exciting delicacy, nonetheless it is not difficult to turn it into good, nourishing and inexpensive meals such as tripe and onions or its rather fancier French equivalent, tripe á la mode de Caen. Crossing the road, we get to The Volunteer,

which is the building at the right-hand edge of the photograph with glazed tiles on the lower half. This old public house became an insurance office in more recent times. The two shops next door both belonged to the Hygienic Bakery, which everybody said used to make cakes like mother used to bake. Both shops changed hands many times as the 21st century approached. Holywell Cross Methodist Church and Chapel have both taken on new roles since this picture was taken: the Methodist Church, which opened here in 1881 after moving from an earlier church off Beetwell Street, was subsequently occupied by Bakers the shopfitters, and the Chapel became the YMCA.

Bottom: Here we are looking north to the mock-Tudor of Knifesmithgate. The bustle of activity on this particular day in 1956 suggests that our snapshot was taken on a Saturday morning. Apart from minor changes, the shops on the left remained much the same throughout the remainder of the 20th century. However, most of the right-hand side has been re-built. Turners department store, on the right-hand corner, closed in 1987 and the site was subsequently taken over by a fast-food chain restaurant. Further up Packers Row, just beyond Turners, was an opening which used to lead to stabling for the horses of Ye Olde Angel, a stage-coach inn of long ago. More recently this site was put to use as a furniture store. The prominent white building facing the camera used to be Pipers' Penny Bazaar in the pre-war years, but by the time of this photograph it had become Paiges, the ladies' outfitters. It was demolished around 1960 along with many other properties, to allow major redevelopment to take place on Burlington Street.

Right: This photograph, taken on a sunny day in 1960, shows a section of Corporation Street which no longer exists. During the second half of the 20th century, Chesterfield's new relief road sliced straight through this corner of the town. At approximately the spot where the cars are parked on the right, a pedestrian footwalk was constructed across the deep cutting that takes the relief road out to join what was, at the time of our picture, the track bed of the Central Railway. The line was closed in 1963. The Hippodrome, seen here on the right, was demolished not long after this photograph was taken. Having begun life as the Theatre Royal as far back as 1886, it became known as The Hippodrome in 1912. Some of the great music hall stars of the era, including Gracie Fields and Sandy Powell, trod the boards here in the theatre's heyday. One of the few buildings on this photograph which has survived is that of The Clifton Hotel, as it was then; it was subsequently known as the Ascot for a short time, and in more recent years became a club called the Barking Badger. Parked at the kerb outside Bernard Lister's Car Mart is a gleaming new Volkswagen Beetle; these cars, with their rear air-cooled engines, were extremely popular in the 1960s and became highly collectible in later years.

Right: This long-established family business was opened in 1903 by John Dent. Chemists shops of the early 20th century used to have their shelves full of enormous and wonderfully picturesque jars and bottles, containing all manner of mysterious medicines and patent concoctions. The pharmaceutical profession and indeed medicine in general evolved dramatically during the course of the century, as modern scientific advances brought us a new and more sophisticated range of drugs and treatments, and also succeeded in developing vaccines to control diseases such as tuberculosis and poliomyelitis which were common in the early decades of the 1900s. It was in 1956, the year in which our photograph was taken, that a newly-developed polio vaccine, having undergone all the necessary trials, became generally available, and parents all over the country queued up to put their children's names down for a vaccination. Dents is still a family-owned business today, although this particular shop was demolished early in the 1960s. Since that time the other shops which we can see beyond Dents on this picture have been replaced by a large, modern building. The traffic lights at the junction have also gone, and the market stalls to the right have been replaced by an open space, furnished with seats and a few trees, where Saturday shoppers are often entertained during the summer months by groups of dancers, Morrismen or bands.

Below left: Barrack Yard, as its name suggests, used to have military connections. These houses in Barrack Yard were once part of the barracks of the Chatsworth Rifles, a militia regiment which was disbanded before 1900. Thereafter they were in civilian occupation until their demolition, providing their residents with an extremely central location, just a few steps away from the town centre amenities. The row of cars parked here is fairly typical of 1959, when the photograph was taken, with a two-tone Rover at the end nearer the camera and the tail fins of either a Ford Zephyr or a Ford Zodiac (the two models were very similar) visible at the other end. There used to be a wide passage off the south side of Vicar Lane, next to Swales shop, which led into this square, and there was also access from Beetwell Street, so Barrack Yard was used by many people as a passageway between Vicar Lane and Beetwell Street. The houses came down around 1963 when Beetwell Street was widened, and after the redevelopment no trace of the old square or its historic buildings was left.

Bottom: Shoppers are enjoying the warm sunshine on this busy Saturday morning in Chesterfield in 1958. Even the motorcyclist is able to enjoy the pleasant breeze in his hair; bikers of this era were not required by law to wear crash helmets. His machine is almost certain to be of British manufacture; among the great British motorcycle manufacturers of those days were names such as Triumph, Enfield, Ariel, Matchless, Francis Barnett, and of course the legendary BSA. Names like Honda, Suzuki, Yamaha and Kawasaki were still virtually unknown in Britain. The early post-war years saw a plentiful supply of army surplus equipment, and Wakefields Army Stores, on the south-east corner of Market Place, was the place to go for well-made, hardwearing clothing for casual or workwear. In particular, army surplus became a popular source of jumpers, footwear, overcoats and gloves, and the store also sold a range of camping equipment and canvas rucksacks. Before Wakefields took this site, part of the premises used to be occupied by Duttons the chemists; and before that, going back more than a hundred years, Chesterfield's very first gas lamp was erected on this corner. Wakefields Army Stores did not see out the 20th century, and the building subsequently housed a branch of the Abbey National Building Society. Next to it on our photograph is Lloyds Bank, which did last out the century.

Right: Here we see the 1975 Whit Walk following its traditional route along Burlington Street. As usual the pavements are thronged with families who have come into town to watch the spectacle. It is a bright morning, although the hats and warm coats worn by the crowd which has gathered outside John Peters on the corner of Burlington Street suggest that the weather was on the chilly side. The parade is led by the Hasland Drum Corps, and they will be followed by the traditional procession of decorated vehicles, bands, and members of the various churches and chapels which take part in this event each year. Prizes are awarded to the best

floats, and the procedure is that floats are judged, and the winner chosen, before the start of the parade. By 1975, the town centre already had designated pedestrian zones, but more changes lay ahead. Woolworth's old building, seen here behind the drummers, was later demolished and replaced by a pedestrian walkway. Further down the street our eyes are drawn to a square building with a distinctive black-and-white side elevation, whose chessboard effect lends it a striking and unfamiliar appearance. The building is actually still there, but is no longer as conspicuous, having been painted white all over.

Above: Overhead, the clouds seem to be gathering rather ominously. An even more ominous sign for the building on the corner next to the traffic lights is the workman, who is busy boarding up the windows of Wraggs of Chesterfield's once-popular motorcycle showroom. It is highly likely that some readers will have bought machines from this spot in their youth; Wraggs always had a good selection of new and used motorbikes, and also supplied Reliant three-wheelers. At the time of our photograph in 1975, Walter Wragg's premises in Lordsmill Street, near the junction with Hasland Road, were already scheduled for demolition along with all the other properties in the foreground. A large roundabout was constructed on the site as part of a major road improvement scheme designed to divert through traffic away from the town centre. When the scheme was finished, this became a major intersection for north-south travellers as well as those going east-west.

Leading off the roundabout was the new relief road, a dual carriageway which enabled northbound through traffic to by-pass the town, looping round it to join the Sheffield Road at Whittington Moor. Another exit from the roundabout took southbound motorists onto a dual carriageway created to carry traffic to the motorway without going through Hasland itself.

Below: This photograph was taken looking down Holywell Street; the road to the left is Newbold Road, and to the right is Sheffield Road. With so little traffic on the road, the notion that within a decade or so this area would be commandeered and turned into a giant car park would have seemed very strange indeed to the citizens whom we see going about their business here in 1959, unaware that they are being captured on film. The Devonshire Arms, on the left, was a very old public house, certainly dating back to at least 1875 as it appears on maps from that year. By 1959, however, its days were numbered. It was demolished around the mid 1960s, when this area changed beyond all recognition. Dolly's shop, next door to the pub, was another victim of the redevelopment which many people were sorry to lose. Dolly's used to be open all hours, even on a Sunday, and being so close to the hospital it was a very handy place for those on their way to visit their loved ones to pop in and buy a little present to cheer the patient up. In the background the square tower of Trinity Church rises up against the horizon; its chancel is the final resting place of George Stephenson, the famous railway engineer.

Below: This view of Holywell Street looking towards Sheffield Road dates from 1960. It was taken on the morning of Whit Monday, and the uniformed figures are members of the St John Ambulance, making their way home after the end of another Whit Walk. This annual procession of decorated floats and bands, organised by local churches and enjoyed by Chesterfield folk of all ages, has a long tradition behind it. In more recent times the date was switched to Spring Bank Holiday Monday. The building seen on the right is Holywell Cross Post Office, which is very old indeed and has been put to many uses over the course of the centuries. We trust that its status as a listed building will ensure its continued preservation. Behind it, Durrant Road leads off to the right. Opposite is Thompson, the Provision Factors, which was another of Chesterfield's old family businesses, and beyond that, a decorator's premises. All these buildings on the left hand side were later pulled down, and a large car park was constructed on the site.

Bottom: With the Market Hall in the background, this is a typical Saturday morning scene, with people out shopping, meeting friends and relations and stopping for a chat. The print dresses of the ladies in the foreground, and the short white ankle socks and sandals of the very young lady, are typical of early 1960s fashion. Our photograph dates from 1963, and as yet there are no signs of rising hemlines. As the 60s progressed, the older generation looked on in horror as their sons wore flowery shirts and grew their hair down past their collar, and their daughters wore mini-skirts, teamed up with knee-high 'wet-look' boots. The 'wet-look' was possible courtesy of the invention of stretch vinyl; wet-look fashion accessories enjoyed great popularity for a while, and no doubt market traders who stocked up with wet-look bags, purses, belts and shoes around that time would have done a good trade - though in retrospect it has to be said that such items were perhaps not in the best of taste. However, we do like the 'hands' of bananas fastened to the cross rail of the stall in the centre of the picture. This very popular greengrocery stall first started in about 1910, on a barrow in New Square. During the second world war, the import of bananas into Britain stopped completely, and for a long time there was not a banana to be seen - so long, in fact, that when it became possible to buy them again, young children had no idea what to do with these strange waxy fruit, and had to be shown how to peel them!

Right: One of the most popular shops on Knifesmithgate, throughout the middle years of the 20th century, was Swallows' department store. Successive generations of Chesterfield families relied upon Swallows for all manner of items, and browsing around the store was a pleasant way to while away your spare time while you were in town, even in the days before the consumer culture became firmly established. This was especially true around Christmas, when Swallows really went to town on its displays, both inside and outside the shop. The decorative, artistic window displays were always colourful and attractive. Christmas saw the upper storey decorated with fairy lights and Father Christmas; our photograph, which dates from December 1960, has captured the atmosphere well, with the festive scene reflected in the wet road. Each year it seemed that a great deal of careful thought had been put into planning the decorations right down to the smallest detail, and passers-by were not slow to express their appreciation. Swallows' Christmas window displays used to be quite a talking-point amongst shoppers, whilst children of all ages could hardly fail to be captivated by the magical scenes and would spend a long time gazing in wonder at each illuminated display in turn. Our picture is likely to bring back considerable nostalgia amongst readers who remember scenes such as this from their younger days. The store was demolished in the early 1970s.

Above: The railway van on the left hand side of Beetwell Street is advertising trips to Blackpool for 13 shillings return (65p in today's currency), giving some indication of the date of the photograph - which in fact is 1958. The shop next to the railway van was the Handymans Stores, a forerunner of modern DIY. The DIY culture had already taken root by 1958, largely as a result of new developments in paints, glues and synthetic building materials, which made products more user-friendly and enabled unskilled and inexperienced workmen - or women - to do their own decorating and home improvements with perfectly adequate results, and more cheaply than if they had called in the professionals. Along from the Handymans Stores, the bow windows belong to the shop of 'Cloggie' Nash, the clog-maker. Continuing down the same side and approaching the corner, a small projecting sign can be seen on an upper storey; from this sign

were suspended three balls, and this marked the shop of Ellse the pawnbroker. There was a convenient short cut through to Vicar Lane around here, where an opening allowed access to Barrack Yard and from there through into Vicar Lane, emerging by Swales shop. All the buildings on the left hand side of Beetwell Street were demolished when the street was widened in the early 1960s.

Below: This popular shopping area has seen many changes in recent years. The building on the right is still there, but has seen a succession of owners come and go. It ended the 20th century as Coopland, the family bakers. On the left, however, everything from Woolworths to the tall building has gone. Woolworths, which had already been part of the Chesterfield shopping scene for at least 30 years when this photograph was taken, moved to the new Vicar Lane shopping complex. Next to Woolworths on this 1959 view is Dobbs the ironmongers, and a very striking feature of their premises was those tall upper windows. It seems that Dobbs had these put in during the early 1900s for a very specific purpose: to enable passengers travelling on the top decks of trams to see the widest possible range of goods on sale inside the shop, as the trams trundled by or halted at the tram-stop outside! Looking further west along Burlington Street, the single storey building behind the car was in fact Cussins Furniture Store, but was still known to local people as the 'Beehive'. Within a couple of years of this photograph, the Beehive had gone, and in fact all these buildings disappeared. Their place was taken by a new road which runs off Burlington Street to connect with Church Lane.

Time in motion

No doubt there were lads in Chesterfield in the 1930s who thought it very unfair that a mere girl should get a chance to ride on the footplate - just because she was the Railway Queen ... This was an era when countless little boys wanted to be engine drivers when they grew up, and no doubt seasoned railwaymen like Driver Stanley Neale and Fireman Norman Bollard, shown on this photograph, grew accustomed to finding themselves surrounded by youngsters who would listen eagerly to all their tales, ask them questions, and tag along behind them in the hopes of being allowed to ride on the footplate. Steam locomotives exercised a fascination all of their own; the basic technology of the steam engine is simple enough to understand, yet that very simplicity seems to add to the sense of wonder and admiration. Most people would probably agree that steam locos had more character than the more sophisticated diesels which replaced them in the 1960s. The metallic smell of the vapour, the rhythmic sound of the engine building up speed, the deafening screech as it let off steam, and the occasional smuts that got into your eyes, were all part of the experience. LMS engine number 372, pictured here, is believed to have been an ex-Midland 4-4-0, originally built between 1882 and 1901 and rebuilt from 1912 onwards. One hundred and sixty-five engines of this class were still in use after nationalisation, but all had been scrapped by 1963.

Left: From the church tower we can look over the top of the Stephenson Memorial Hall and down Corporation Street. Erected by public subscription and opened in 1879, the Stephenson Memorial Hall was subsequently taken over by the Corporation and became the Civic Theatre, Library and Information Centre. It was one of the first places in Chesterfield to show moving pictures. The awnings on the left hand side of the bend just below us belong to the India tyre business, which opened at 16 Corporation Street in the summer of 1929. The anatomy of the motor car was no doubt quite a mystery to most people in those early days of motoring, and we feel that the mechanics amongst our readership might be intrigued by some of India Super Tyres' opening offers. For instance, they recommended Heatproof Blue Tubes, and they also offered to convert your old Beaded Edge High Pressure Tyres to BALLOON low pressure tyres. This conversion would, they promised, give you twice the comfort and thrice the mileage. To the left of India Super Tyres is the Hippodrome, and further away from the camera is the Station Hotel, now renamed the Chesterfield, with the taxi offices and Winfields Builders Merchants to the right. Not only has the station building seen here been replaced, but even its replacement has been replaced.

Below: No collection of photographs of Chesterfield in days gone by would be complete without a picture of St James's Hall in Vicar Lane. Fondly remembered by many of the older generation as Jimmy's, this establishment was officially known as the Chesterfield Dance Centre during the 1940s and 50s. Before that, the hall had been used for numerous church activities, meetings, concerts and parties, and it could also be hired for private functions. Carved into the lintel over one of the doorways was the inscription: Erected by Cecil Littleton, Vicar of this Parish, AD 1896, in memory of his mother. - and a very effective way of perpetuating the memory of his mother it was, too: countless thousands of people must have passed by and read those words, over the years. Jimmy's finally closed in the late 1980s, and around a decade later the whole of Vicar Lane was flattened and Jimmy's vanished along with the rest. New shops were subsequently erected on the site, and nothing of the old Vicar Lane survived into the 21st century apart from the name, and the memories which still linger on in the minds of those who remember this part of Chesterfield as it used to be.

This photograph was taken in New Square in 1939 or 1940, and records a delivery of gas masks to Chesterfield. Gas attack was what the country dreaded. Millions of gas masks were manufactured, and the government took steps to ensure that every citizen was issued with their own gas mask, which it was then their responsibility to look after. For babies, there were anti-gas attack suits. Younger children were issued with Mickey Mouse masks, which were less frightening for them. Demonstrations were held to show people how to put the masks on and use them, and we all knew that we must carry them with us at all times - as the posters said, Hitler

would send no warning. House-to-house checks were sometimes carried out to make sure that every member of the household had a serviceable gas mask and knew where it was, and some cinemas and other public buildings had a policy of refusing to admit anybody who did not have their gas mask with them. Of course, as the war progressed and no gas ever materialised, we became a bit more casual about our masks. And the boxes, if you took the mask out, made such handy containers for sandwiches ... Gas mask cartons were manufactured by Robinsons Box Division, who during the war supplied nearly four and a half million of them.

Bottom : Not a classic car rally, but an official police parade which we believe was staged towards the end of the second world war, when the Home Secretary visited Chesterfield. The fine MG roadster heading the procession is carrying Inspector Barnet. Car headlamps have been blacked out to comply with blackout restrictions, and bumpers painted white to help avoid accidents. Local papers such as the Derbyshire Times used to print 'dim-out times' instead of 'lighting-up times', and people got accustomed to travelling in the dark. Strategic sections of the kerb and potential obstacles such as lamp-posts, railings and trees were picked out with white markings to help travellers; the far kerb on this photograph appears to have received this treatment. Official visits during wartime were shrouded in secrecy. No publicity was given to the movements of the royal family and other leading statesmen, for reasons of security, and normally the only bystanders at such events, if any, would be random clusters of spectators who happened to be passing, noticed that something was going on, and stopped to watch. Similarly, official reports of enemy bombing raids were deliberately vague, leaving listeners and readers to make educated guesses about the exact location. Reports often referred to 'a town in the Midlands' (which was likely to mean Birmingham or Coventry), 'a city in the north of England' (all too often, Sheffield) or 'a city in the south' (probably London).

Right: Horns Bridge Way is pictured here in 1930, two years before the old bridge over Hasland Road was replaced by a new steel girder bridge. In fact three railway lines crossed here; the two that are visible are the East Coast railway, which is labelled Dukeries Route, and the LMS main line running

from the North to London. The invisible third line is the Central, running below the road in a tunnel. It was quite a feat of engineering. The stone skew bridge which carried the Midland line over the road was erected in 1839 by George Stephenson himself, arguably the greatest of the Victorian railway engineers, who lived in Chesterfield from 1837 until his death in 1848. The reasons for replacing the 90-year-old bridge had nothing to do with the integrity of the structure itself; engineers agreed that, all things being equal, it would have been good for another 90 years at least. But the Corporation wanted to widen Hasland Road, and the bridge was by that time carrying some 400 trains a day, both passenger and goods, which it had not been designed for, and would soon have required strengthening. So it was decided to build a completely new bridge, and within a couple of years of this photograph the advertising hoardings were gone, the road was wider and safer with a separate walkway for pedestrians and a better view of oncoming traffic, and one way and another this spot looked very different. By the end of the 20th century it looked different again, with a large traffic roundabout and the high-level bridge removed following the closure of the East Coast line.

By 1956, people were becoming enthusiastic about the potential of helicopter travel. When the Duke of Edinburgh presented the prizes at Welbeck College's Speech Day that year, he dropped in by helicopter. Our photograph shows a demonstration sponsored by Markhams, the mining engineers. Markhams were exploring the possibility of using helicopters when visiting collieries outside a 40 mile radius. They calculated that, for instance, it took two and a half hours to get to Coventry by road, which was a distance of 72 miles - no M1 in those days! - whereas by helicopter the trip would take less than half an hour. So they arranged for Westland to test a proposed airfield site at Sill Over

Hill. So one Sunday in July 1956 this Westland Wigeon five-seater helicopter duly spent more than half an hour landing and taking off in one of the fields on the proposed site, and the conclusion was that the field would be fine for light aircraft. The Mayor, Alderman W Weston, and his Deputy, Alderman H C Day, were among the guests who took a trial trip, and it is on record that this was the first time either of them had flown. The general consensus was that the site, one mile to the east of the town centre, was very accessible, and the stability of the aircraft was impressive. However, helicopters are not cheap to buy; even in those days a Wessex Wigeon would have cost somewhere in the region of £30,000.

Above: Of all the buildings seen here, only the Alliance building survived the 1970s demolition programme. Developments which took place around that time resulted in the car park in Elder Way next to the Alliance Building Society disappearing, along with the houses behind it, to make way for a large Co-op grocery store and offices. However, there had to be a car park; as we can see in this 1961 photograph, people needed somewhere to park their cars and motor cycles. So the buildings on the far side, as we look across to Saltergate, were in their turn pulled down to make space for a public car park, much larger than the one seen here in the foreground. The shop with the dark doorway, beyond the cars, used to be a boot repair shop which was patronised by many Chesterfield people. The opening at the left hand side of the shop was Dobbs Yard, and at the end of the opening there used to be a row of very old cottages.

Right: We have no precise date for this photograph, but we believe it may date from around the end of the second world war. During the wartime, an evening curfew was imposed on the bus service. This was lifted in October 1944, and Chesterfield was able to claim the distinction of being the first town to keep its buses running until 10 o'clock at night, taking advantage of the relaxing of restrictions - a welcome sign that things were beginning to return to normal. That same year, the British Omnibus Company's Public Relations Committee published this astonishingly poetic advertisement: 'The most harassing day must come to an end; the longest one has its evening. And then the recuperative peace of home, the lazy relaxation, the restoration of nerves and brain! But for the buses these intervals of ease would be shorter; private lives would lose an element of that precious element - time.' Modern cynics in Chesterfield might argue that nerves and brain would become somewhat less frayed, and require less restoration, if the town had a proper bus station. Then you wouldn't have to tire your brain working out where your next bus went from, and get all harassed dashing across town to catch it!

At the shops

his very old photograph has been preserved in the form of a postcard bearing a 1904 postmark. It is fascinating to see Market Hall surrounded by horsedrawn traffic; the classically simple style of the building gives it a timeless quality, so that it never looks out of place. Careful examination of our photograph reveals the words 'Houston, Chemist' on the shop to the left of the main market entrance. Directories from that year list Frederick John Houston as 'chemist and druggist', with premises at 20 Market Hall and also in South Street, New Whittington. He was also 'proprietor of Houston's gripe and blood

purifying mixtures' and other household remedies including 'ivy leaf corn silk.' When it came to selling products to purify the blood, Mr Houston had many competitors, such as Clarke's Blood Mixture, which remained popular for decades. Other pills and potions of the day included Martin's Pills, Beecham's Pills, Carter's Little Liver Pills which promised to cure problems such as torpid liver, sallow skin and furred tongue, and Toko which was designed to cure, among other things, indigestion and nervous prostration. No doubt Mr Houston had a good selection of patent concoctions such as these in his Market Hall shop.

Below centre: This effective snapshot was taken looking into a sunny New Square, through the arches of T P Woods' wine shop. This flourishing business was opened in 1844, and continued as a landmark in the town until it was sold to a brewery company around 1910. T P Woods himself was a hard-working man, and the interests of Chesterfield were dear to his heart. He went on to become a councillor, and subsequently held the office of Mayor on more than one occasion. It seems that T P Woods was the driving force behind the town's decision to purchase part of Maynards Meadows and establishing the layout of Queen's Park to mark the diamond jubilee of Queen Victoria. Later on, Woods' wine shop disappeared, and the site was taken over and redeveloped into a Littlewoods store.

road had to be diverted away from the town centre because of the volume of traffic using this route, and New Square was closed to through traffic. The stalls have also been moved and now stand next to the Market Hall, but here we see the stalls in their old position, set out all ready for market day. Adjoining Dents to the right is the Star & Garter Inn; this establishment was already closed at the time when our photograph was taken, and from this angle there is no name visible, although the lettering would still have been visible on the side elevation. To the left of Dents we can just catch a glimpse of the Market Place Station. This had once been a passenger station, but towards the end of its life it was used as a goods station only, and it was demolished around the end of the 1960s. The Portland and the buildings to the right have escaped demolition, but the rest have been replaced by tall, modern retail and office premises.

Bottom: In 1953, when this picture was taken, the main thoroughfare from West Bars carried on through New Square to the High Street. Later, the

The Market Hall has been very much at the heart of Chesterfield life for around a century and a half; this typical scene of bustling activity was captured by the camera in 1952. Built from local brick, the hall was opened in 1857 by a private business concern, the Chesterfield Market Company. The company had invested the grand total of £13,350 in the venture, including the purchase of the market rights and other associated legal expenses. Prior to that, Chesterfield had been without a market hall for more than 50 years, the previous one having been demolished towards the end of the 18th century after falling into disrepair. The new covered market originally measured 55 yards by 30 yards and had 25

stalls and 25 perimeter shops; upstairs was the Corn Exchange, a large assembly room and a number of offices. Market Hall was acquired by the Council in 1874, and thereafter various refurbishment, improvement and modernisation schemes have been carried out to keep the market facilities in tune with the needs of shoppers, whilst at the same time preserving the character of Market Place. In 1954, £7,600 was invested in reorganising the stalls and providing more retail accommodation. A further major refurbishment programme took place around 1980, when central heating was installed; as a result, the chimneys which we see on this photograph became redundant, and were removed.

Left: A number of familiar old names can be picked out on this view of High Street from Market Place, dated 1966. Snelsons, MacFisheries, Marks & Spencer, Swallows, Boots and the Home & Colonial are all trading, while the hoarding just this side of MacFisheries announces that Marks & Spencers have recently acquired the site that used to be Hadfield & Sons Pork and Provision Merchant, established 1859. Many of the 20th century's most successful retail chains were started by one or two individuals, and were subsequently built up over the decades into giant retail chains with one branch or more in virtually every shopping area in the country. So, for instance, Boots was started by Nottingham's Jesse Boot, Woollies by the American brothers Woolworth, and Marks & Sparks by Mr Michael Marks and Mr Tom Spencer. M&S began trading as the Penny Bazaar, and Woolworths, known in America as the '5 and 10 cent Stores', was introduced to Britain with the tag of '3d and 6d Stores'. MacFisheries, however, began rather differently. This chain was established by the philanthropist Lord Leverhulme, who during the early 1920s developed a project to help the impoverished Scottish crofters. He helped them set up as fishermen, and in order to provide an outlet for the fish they caught, he bought 300 shops throughout the country, which traded as MacFisheries.

Above: Transformations are under way in New Square; Dents the Chemist and the old Star & Garter public house have gone, and work has started on the new building for Dents. The year is 1962. The people of Chesterfield looked on with interest as the new building took shape and grew up around the crane. Then, when the building was almost complete, this crane was lifted out section by section by an even larger, mobile crane. It was all change in Chesterfield around this time; more construction work and yet another crane can be seen in the background towards the left of our picture, where work is in progress on the new building for the Accountant General's Department of the Post Office. Of the two structures, Dents' New Square premises are still there, while the AGD building had a very short lifespan indeed and was demolished in 1997, due to serious structural defects. Fortunately for the town, the Post Office decided to stay in Chesterfield, and in due course another Post Office building was put up.

For a period around the 1960s, Chesterfield's Market Hall was shorn of its dome top and, as we can see here, it looked decidedly bald and a little comical. We believe this photograph to have been taken in 1968. Many years elapsed between the removal of the original dome and the installation of the fibreglass replacement dome which Market Hall has worn ever since. On our photograph, a large hoarding advertises £25,000 Jackpot Prizes, and we wonder how many of the keen-eyed shoppers, caught on camera as they hunt for a bargain, have invested a pound in a Premium Bond. Premium Bonds are more fondly known as Ernies, so-called after the Electronic Random Number Indicator used to select the winning numbers. The first £5,000 prize draw took place on 1st June, 1957. For just £1, you could cheer yourself up by thinking of all the things you would do when your Ernie came up. By the end of the 20th century we had the National Lottery, with all its hype, and in all its various forms of evolution - twice weekly draws, roll-overs, scratch cards, lucky dips and so forth. Ernies are much simpler and less stressful: all you have to do is buy a bond, put it in a safe place, and keep your fingers firmly crossed.

Making a living

Most readers will be familiar with this cottage, although it might not be instantly recognisable ... Revolution House is being rethatched, in May 1946. Three hundred years ago, this cottage in the village of Whittington was an alehouse named the Cock and Pynot (a pynot is a magpie); an old picture from those days shows it as a long, low building. In 1688 it was a secret venue where plans were made for the revolution that would depose the unpopular - and Catholic - James II from the throne. Perhaps surprisingly, little interest was then taken in the place which played such a significant part in the revolution until shortly before the bi-centenary of the hatching of the plot, in 1888.

By that time the inn had become a private cottage and fallen into disrepair. The cottage was renovated, although the room believed to have been the actual 'plotting chamber' was beyond rescue. Great celebrations were held; the village was decorated for the occasion, there was a firework display, the poor were treated to a tea in the Lower Corn Exchange, and a banquet was held in Market Hall and included such delicacies as devilled eels for starters and Matrimonial jelly for dessert. Thereafter Revolution House has been properly looked after, and was refurbished again around the time of the Tercentenary celebrations in 1988, when a new audio-visual room was opened by HRH The Prince of Wales.

Below: We're not quite sure why everybody looks so happy - perhaps it's because the sun is out, or perhaps they just enjoy working at Robinsons. The photograph was taken in 1939 - which of course was the firm's centenary year - outside the Waffa Works. In that year the firm's workforce totalled 3,454, of whom 56 were, by the December, away on active service with the armed forces. War or no war, spirits seem to be high if we can judge by the smiling faces and jaunty poses on our picture, and indeed those who had the good fortune to be employed by Robinsons enjoyed many advantages throughout the 20th century. One of the popular things during the 1930s was Benefit Clubs; this became almost a craze around that time, and a great many Clubs were started up at Robinsons (though we do not know how many of them managed to keep going during the war). There was, for instance, the Shoe Club; so some of these well-shod ladies will probably have paid in a shilling a week to get a new pair of shoes. A good pair of ladies' court shoes at the time cost 8/11. Other clubs included the Towel Club, the Pot Club, the Hairdressing Club and the Chocolate Club; the idea, of course, was to help people budget or save up for certain items in the medium term, at a time when practically everybody was paid weekly, in cash.

Right: Dressed in their best, these ladies are off to London. The occasion is the Centenary of the founding of Robinsons in 1839, and, to celebrate, the firm treated employees and their families to an all-expenses-paid day out in the capital. Eight special LMS trains were chartered to transport around 3,700 people, with the first train scheduled to leave Chesterfield at 4.22 am. The care which had gone into planning the trip down to the last detail was typical of the company's thoughtful attitude towards its workforce. Morning papers were provided on the train, everybody was given a first-class breakfast, and ladies could have their hair done - no doubt a very welcome facility for those who had had to leave the house before four in the morning! From St Pancras, groups were ferried around in a fleet of 80 buses which took them on a tour of London, with stops for refreshment at various Lyons Corner House restaurants. Arrangements had been made in advance for luncheons and teas to be served, along with orchestral accompaniment. After tea, people were free to amuse themselves until evening, when they all had seats for a Grand Variety Concert at the Albert Hall. They then returned to Chesterfield, with supper on the train; the last group arrived back at 4.56 am. The bill for the day reportedly came to £7,215.4s.5d. It was an unqualified success - any readers who went on the trip are sure to remember it, while others will doubtless have heard about it from their parents.

Looking south-west over Chesterfield from the top of the Town Hall, we can pick out a number of tall industrial chimneys which used to be such a striking feature of the panorama. By the end of the 20th century, none of them was left standing. The chimney towards the centre, below the puff of white steam, belonged to Wheatbridge Mill. Built by Robinsons in 1876, Wheatbridge Mill remained standing for 120 years, although it ceased operating as a mill nine years before it was demolished. The old Brampton Brewery, which is the tall tower block on the right, was also pulled down, and the site was subsequently redeveloped as a large retail complex. The left-hand foreground, which was given over to allotments at the time of the photograph in 1954, has since been landscaped and incorporates a modern courthouse which was constructed in the early 1960s.

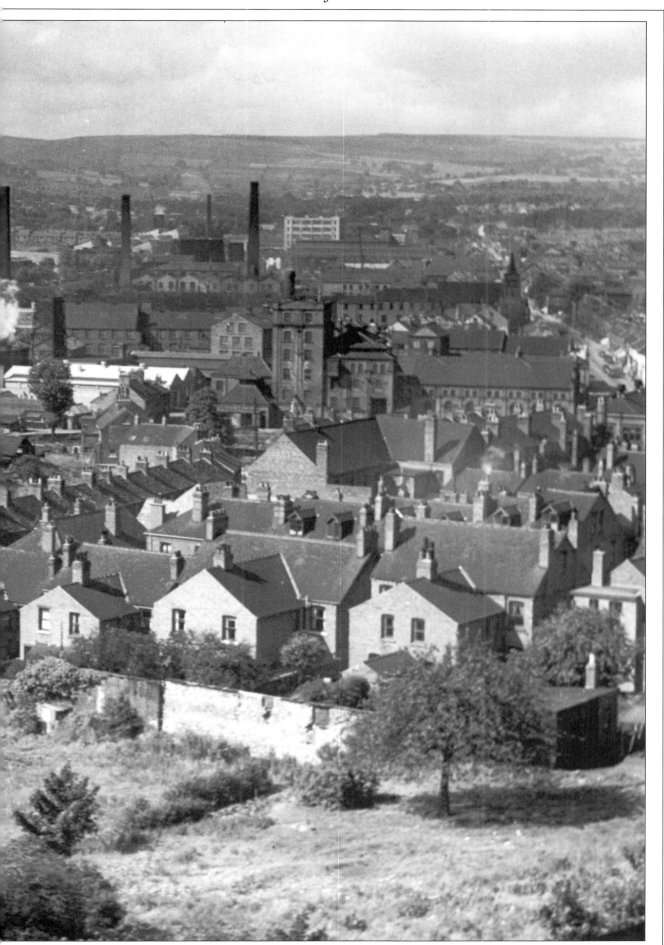

Bottom: This atmospheric photograph of Robinson's Wheatbridge Mill was taken at around half past four on a winter's afternoon in, we think, 1956. With lights blazing in all the windows and the outline of the mill itself very stark and black against the sunset, the result is very dramatic indeed; it almost looks as though the entire building is ablaze. The mill was built in 1876, and over the years provided employment for many thousands of Chesterfield people. The tall chimney which rises in silhouette against the evening sky was built in 1895, and stood just over 140 feet high. It was demolished in 1973. Wheatbridge Mill closed down in 1987 and was finally pulled down in 1996. To many local people, its demolition marked the end of an era. The site was subsequently transformed into a retail park.

Right: Newbold Back Lane can be seen on the left-hand side of this photograph and shows the view looking across towards the two trees seen here over the roof of the farm building. The heap of rubble in front of the farm is the result of roadworks which in fact mark the start of what was to become Loundsley Green Road, connecting Newbold and Ashgate. The old farm itself was to disappear, and the land was to become the site of a hotel, set further back from the road than the farm buildings used to be. The hotel was originally called The Olde House, but it subsequently became The Trading Post. Its immediate surroundings changed more than a little, too; housing estates sprang up all around it, and this became a densely populated residential area.

The date given for this splendid photograph of the Sheepbridge Foundry Engineering Department is 1st January, 1935, and clearly the manufacture of bomb casings is under way. Around that time the government was focusing on its re-armament programme for military aircraft, and this provided plenty of work for Sheepbridge FED. In fact, we understand that the Air Ministry financed the construction of a complete new engineering shop, with machinery installed to produce 3" ML HE bomb forgings. Additional plant was provided by the Air Ministry to machine 3.7" anti-aircraft shells. Overall the foundry made a tremendous contribution to the war effort. Prior to becoming involved in the armament programme, it had manufactured items such as cast pipes for water and sanitation, and, during the 1920s, centrifugal castings for the growing motor car and aircraft industries. The longstanding connection with Stokes, the Mansfield manufacturer of motor car cylinders, dates back to that time. However, the origins of the Sheepbridge company go right back to the mid 19th century, and the ironworks is believed to have been one of the wave of new industrial ventures set up all over Britain in the wake of the Great Exhibition of 1851. In those days coal mining was thriving around Dunston, Whittington, Barlow and Sheepbridge; new houses were built for the workers, and so the settlement of Sheepbridge grew up around the mines.

Left: This man is demonstrating the base-forming operation used for small cylinders at Chesterfield Tube Company in 1965 - a precision task which clearly required skill and concentration. The Tube Works celebrated its 100th anniversary in 1997. We understand the methods used changed surprisingly little over the course of that century. The company was set up under the formidable name of The Universal Weldless Steel Tube Company (Ehrhardt's Process), with the modest aim of making between two and three thousand tubes a week, destined primarily for use as boiler tubes on the warships of the Royal Navy. The firm was officially renamed The Chesterfield Tube Company in 1906 and kept this name until 1966 - though locally it always has and probably always will be known simply as The Tube Works. The Tube Works subsequently moved into the manufacture of high quality, seamless steel high pressure gas cylinders,

and went on to dominate this market. During the second world war, production focused on military equipment, including miles and miles of tubing for Sten gun barrels. Readers who had connections with the Tube Works around that time are likely to remember Joseph Hicks Langford Trevorrow, who was in charge of the firm before and during the war; his successor, Dennis Lacy-Hulbert, took over in the late 1940s. More recently the company became United Engineering Forgings Limited.

Below: The co-existence of the Regal Cinema and the overhead trolleybus cables help pinpoint the date of this photograph within a couple of years. Trolleybuses operated in Chesterfield between 1927 and 1938, while the Regal was opened towards the end of 1936. We can therefore safely say that this snapshot was taken between 1936 and 1938, when the Regal was still

relatively new and the trolleybuses were almost at the end of their allotted span. Many trolleybus enthusiasts feel that these vehicles came to a premature and undeserved end, and that the decision to scrap them was taken too hastily. The actual properties in the photograph have remained largely unaltered over the years, although the businesses which occupy them have changed. To the right of the roadworks is the building which was constructed around 1910 as a branch of the Manchester-based Williams and Deacons Bank. It was designed by a Chesterfield architect, Mr Cecil Jackson, and a thriving local building firm of the day, J Collis & Sons, was responsible for its construction. The building is still a bank at the time of writing, though no longer Williams Deacons. Next to it, away from the camera, is Hoyle's, described in the contemporary local directories as a 'costumier'. Opposite the bank we see Mason's tobacconists shop, well situated for passing trade. Mason's had another outlet in the Market Hall.

In April 1936 the Mayor laid the foundation stone for Chesterfield's new Town Hall, and by 30th July the structure had begun to take shape, as we can see from this photograph of the building works taken from Market Hall. The overall development cost around £173,000, although the Town Hall building itself accounted for only £146,500 of that amount. The general opinion was that it was worth every penny; as Councillor Kirk said, it was 'a good job, a good site and a good layout.' However, the money had to be found from somewhere, and so it was calculated that the actual cost to the people of Chesterfield would work out at fivepence in the pound on the rates for the next 60 years - so according to those projections, we would have just nicely finished paying our dues in time to start the third millennium. It becomes apparent from looking at old newspapers that some concerns are common to every generation, with rates being one of them. The rate for 1938-9 was kept at the same level as the previous year - 14/6 (73p in new money) - but the fixing of the rate had been the subject of grave and lengthy discussions in Council that year. It was agreed that drastic economies must be made in years to come; if not, Chesterfield could find itself heading for a 17/-, or even - horror of horrors - an 18/- rate. And that, everybody agreed, would be a very serious matter indeed.

Above: This large, modern, very 60s-looking building was in fact constructed in 1963 for a department of the Post Office. The decision to locate the AGD offices in Chesterfield was good news for the town's economy. Many staff were moved up from the London area, and a special housing estate was built at Loundsley Green to accommodate them. However, it seems that there were structural problems inherent in the block, to which there was no solution other than to demolish it, and this was duly done in 1997. Another Post Office building, of a more traditional design, now occupies the same site. This photograph was taken by Mr Martin from across Queens Park lake as a winter's afternoon was drawing to a close, and he has used the fading light to blur the lines of the building behind the delicate silhouettes of the trees and the soft reflections in the water. In fact, we think he has succeeded in making this plain, angular structure look as attractive as a functional concrete office is ever likely to look.

Above centre: Remember the days before everything came pre-packed? When the grocer weighed out your butter to order, and biscuits and sweets came out of big jars behind the counter? Kiddies' mouths would begin to water as they watched the sales assistant scoop the sweets out in a metal scoop, weigh them, and slide them out of the scoop into those little paper bags. Some old favourites can be picked out on this photograph: there are Barley Sugar Sticks, Coffee Crunch and Blackcurrant with Vitamin C, along with more modern varieties like Kola. On the counter are pre-packed tubes of Chocolate Mints - an indication that the packaging industry is already beginning to come into its own. Trebor was founded in 1907, and added mints to its range of boiled sweets in 1935; many readers will remember the TV jingle 'Trebor Mints are a Minty Bit Stronger'. It is said that the word Trebor was carved on the house where the original factory was set up; this seemed a good omen, as it spells Robert backwards and one of the two founders was named Robert Robertson. So Robertson and Woodcock's business took the name Trebor. The hairdo of the smiling saleslady gives us a clue as to the date of our photograph - without the cap, her hair would no doubt be done up in the 'beehive' that was so popular in the 60s, and, sure enough, the year is 1965.

Marketing glamour

Psst!! Want to buy a show girl's feather head dress? Or maybe rent a stretch limo? And where do both Jimmy Cricket and Bernie Clifton's ostrich look for their shoes? Where on earth might one look to get hold of such an unusual collection of goods? The answer is simple: Dapet Textiles of Chesterfield, a firm which with some confidence today challenges its many customers to find a wider choice of theatrical goods at a more competitive price.

Dapet Textiles traces its origins to the early 1960s when Peter Selley, a civil engineer, decided to start selling fabrics from a market stall. Peter was prompted to go it alone when his next engineering contract would have forced him to work abroad.

Selling fabrics from a market stall at that time was very difficult, not least since it was quite hard even to get on to a market. Peter Selley had to start by being a casual trader, not occupying the same position every day. Appropriately the original name of the business was Peter's Textiles.

It was hard work in the cold and wet - vehicles sometimes broke down and markets were often moved as towns were redeveloped. The first market stall was at Matlock, but the business gradually expanded to include Chesterfield, Retford and Leicester as well as Eckington which in those days had an evening market. Eventually running several market stalls, Peter Selley and his family found themselves needing to keep three vans just to take stock to the markets.

Peter's wife Rosa, sadly now deceased, helped out as much as possible whilst working full time. Today there are three generations involved in the business: Peter and Rosa's son, David Selley, runs the wholesale business,

Above left: *Founder, Peter Selley.*
Below: *The firm's first premises.*

David's wife Linda runs the factory whilst David and Linda's children Brendon, Mandy and Nikki all work full time in the company warehouse. And Peter Selley himself, now confined to a wheelchair, also still comes in once or twice a week.

Peter and David Selley worked the markets for 28 years until Dapet Textiles was established. During that time they also ran a textile shop on Dale Road in Matlock.

The new business, taking its name from an amalgam of David and Peter, was started at 282 Chatsworth Road, Chesterfield in 1983 with the main aim of supplying specialist theatrical fabrics to dance schools. The Selleys only ceased trading on markets in 1990 when Dapets had become a sucessful business. The Chatsworth Road premises were extended to 280 around 1988.

Today the business is miles removed from market stalls - everything is computerised with all the latest technology being employed at the Dapet factory to manufacture dance wear.

Uniquely in Britain the firm specialises in selling theatrical fabrics, for example supplying most British holiday centres such as Butlins, Pontins, Haven Holidays and Oasis as well as entertainers, television, theatres and all types of shows from village halls to the West End productions, in addition to the original dancing schools. Well known customers include Alton Towers, Blackpool Pleasure Beach shows, Tussauds and Chessington World of Adventure.

Abroad, textiles are supplied to cruise liners, including all of the P&O line, holiday centres in the USA, theatres, touring shows and casinos. Materials and costumes have been sold to many famous productions such as 'Lord of the Dance' and 'Feet of Flames' which marked the retirement of Michael Flatley from dancing. 150 British pantos are supplied with fabrics every year on top of theatrical productions such as Grease, Fame and Jolson.

Above and above left: *The firm's second premises at Chatsworth Road.* ***Below:*** *The factory.*

Dapet staff attend many fittings for these shows, employees travelling the length and breadth of England.

Fabrics from Dapet Textiles have appeared on TV's the Generation Game, Last of the Summer Wine, Stars in Their Eyes and many other series. Television stars and personalities who have been dressed in Dapet fabrics are innumerable but include Frank Bruno, Barry Cryer, Bonnie Langford, Bucks Fizz Jeremy Beadle, Michael Barrymore and Rick Wakeman.

Many touring circuses too rely on Dapet Textiles to send them fabulous fabrics. And cinema too has provided a major market with the firm supplying fabrics to the film industry including the latest Star Wars film.

Glitzy glamorous fabrics from Dapets can cost from a mere £1 per metre up to £3,000 a metre and the company will also happily supply ready-made dance wear, dancing shoes, feathers and head dresses. The firm will sell any quantity from one to a thousand garments to a customer, with many exotic fabrics being specially imported for the business. The company uses only the best machinery to manufacture dance wear and only imports the best quality fabrics available from a variety of countries around the world.

Staff will famously go out of their way to meet show deadlines and all the firm's employees are well trained in all aspects of the Dapet business; many of them are also experienced in theatrical work themselves.

In addition to theatrical fabrics the business also has a bridal wear department, a curtaining department, a full pointe shoe fitting service as well as providing dance wear, dance shoes and ballroom shoes - in addition to offering professional advice on such delicate topics as fitting show

*Above centre: A caricature of three generations of the family. From left to right: Peter, David and Brendon. **Right:** Jimmy Cricket decides on his next pair of stage shoes. **Below:** Two of the fleet of Dream Cars (Derbyshire) Ltd.*

girl outfits and the management of feather head dresses. It seems Dapet Textiles, which also incorporates Stagedoor Fabrics and the Chesterfield Dancewear Centre, can supply anything from wigs, to rubber masks, theatrical makeup through to hats and flags. You name it- they've got it, and got it in abundance. So much material is supplied by Dapet Textiles that it is almost impossible that any reader of this book will not have personally seen some of its products either on television or at a live show.

But not content with their unusual, indeed unique, business the Selley family is now embarking upon yet anther business venture: Dream Cars (Derbyshire) Ltd with a fleet of Rolls Royces and stretch limousines for all types of weddings and chauffeur services.

It's all a far cry from a wet market day in Matlock all those years ago when, the no doubt nervous, Peter Selley set out a new course for his life, abandoning the relative security and certainty of a civil engineer's life for the insecurity and uncertainty of life as a market trader. Little could he have foreseen just how his life would change and the direction the business would eventually take in the following years.

Locally made ice-cream that takes some licking

Ice-cream. What can beat an ice cream on a warm summer's day after a walk in the hills? Legend has it that the first Englishman to eat ice cream was Richard the Lion Heart who was introduced to the then extraordinary luxury by his great Muslim opponent in the Holy Land, the more than chivalrous Saladin. How Saladin managed to get ice in the hot lands of the middle east is not recorded.

Ice-cream was not to become a regular feature of life for ordinary mortals until the latter half of the 19th century, when Italians introduced it to this country, despite having enjoyed popularity as a luxury dessert in Paris some two hundred years earlier.

In 1998 one of Chesterfield's legendary firms celebrated 100 years in the business - Frederick's Ice Cream based in Old Hall Road, Brampton. Not many towns can boast about having a local ice-cream maker, let alone one that still produces ice-cream to the original 1898 recipe that still wins awards today. In fact the business is even older than that, having been begun by one Angelo, an Italian farmer and ice-cream maker who came to England in the 1870s, although his name only appeared in White's Sheffield business directory in 1898. He was one of the first vendors to introduce the traditional style of Italian ice-cream to the working classes, giving them their first frozen experience many years before the days of electricity and refrigeration and the mass produced ice-creams of today. The founder was born in Parma in Northern Italy and started his own ice-cream business in the Paradise Lane area of Sheffield.

That Angelo did not speak English was a problem, but like so many of his compatriots of the period Angelo soon learned enough to sell his ice-cream, and like them introduced us to such Italianisms as Tutti Frutti - all fruit, and the 'Hokey Pokey' man. This phrase goes back to the days when the Italian ice-cream street vendors would break off a wafer and scoop a small amount of ice-cream onto it for the children to try with the words "ecco un poco" (here is a little) - the children picked up the phrase and christened the early ice-cream men as 'Hokey Pokey' men. Their hand carts were brightly painted and decorated

Above: John Russell outside the Star & Garter Yard in the 1930s. **Below:** *Bruno Frederick is on the far right of this 1950s picture.*

in gold leaf and would have seemed like a mirage to the children who lived in the dimly lit cobbled streets of the late industrial revolution.

Another problem in those days was keeping ice-cream cold without domestic refrigerators. In winter, some ice-cream makers would collect ice from frozen ponds to help keep their wares frozen but following the invention of the ice-making machine in America ice blocks could be bought from industrial suppliers. In those days milk and cream from the farm were hand turned before the days of electricity. Frederick's ice-cream is still made by hand but helped by electrical ice-cream making machines from Italy.

During those very early times Angelo, assisted by his wife and son, worked to develop his original 1898 blend of Italian ice-cream. The same traditional brands of Vanilla

and Dairy ices are still being made and sold by Frederick's today.

Four generations of the family would eventually be involved in the ice-cream business, five of whom still work in it today.

Links with Chesterfield go back to 1925 when Angelo's son John, who traded under the name of John Russell, moved to Chesterfield and established his own business in the Star and Garter Yard, New Square before moving to the present headquarters in Old Hall Road, Brampton in 1947, two years after the end of the second world war.

During the war food was rationed, farmer's milk supplies were stopped and ice-cream making was seriously affected. Despite such difficulties John Russell, who became an air raid warden for the duration of the war, struggled to carry on.

The business became known as Frederick's in the 1950s after John Russell's daughter Pauline married Bruno Frederick whose own family had been in the ice-cream business in Atherton since the 1900s. Fredericks ice-cream was originally

Top: A trailer in Market Square in the 1960s. *Above:* A Morris Commerical van from 1953, restored by the company in the 1990s. *Left:* The Frederick family. From left to right: Pauline, Julie, Bruno and Louise Taaffe.

sold around Atherton from hand-carts and later from horse-drawn carts. Still surviving within the firm to this day is an original Z-type Morris van and a mid-Victorian horse-drawn cart from 1873. This has recently been restored to its original condition and is on display to the public.

In the mid 1950s the firm became a member of the National Ice Cream Alliance. Membership established Frederick's Traditional Ice Cream on a national register and allowed the firm to compete with the best ice-cream makers in the United Kingdom.

Over the years the company has gained award after award, including three times winner of the Best Ice-Cream in Britain as well as numerous medals and over 70 diplomas and, as a consequence, is now more than entitled to advertise its product as 'Award Winning Ice Cream'.

Today the company's main market covers both local outlets and the Peak District, selling to the general public and tourists as well as supermarkets and shops. Tourists and walkers rightly love Frederick's ice-creams which, apart from their delicious taste and cooling nature, are uniquely valuable as an excellent slow energy release food providing a steady source of energy for today's busy lifestyles, walking, leisure activities or even shopping.

Bruno and Pauline Frederick are now senior executive partners in the firm helped by their son and two daughters.

Frederick's has become well known as sponsors and suppliers of the Bakewell Show, the Angling Fair, Ashover Show, Chatsworth International Horse Trials, Chatsworth Country Fair, Belvoir Castle and Holkham Country Fair. Once the business was conducted entirely from mobile ice-cream vans and carts. Today everything is much more permanent with vans and kiosks scattered throughout the Peak District on licensed

sites owned or managed by the local Council, the Peak National Park, the National Trust and English Heritage. The company works closely with the National Trust and Hardwick Hall. One unusual commission received by the firm was to produce 'Elizabethan Ice Cream' to celebrate the 400th Anniversary of Hardwick Hall.

Special commissions are nothing unusual for Frederick's which has also produced its 'Spirite Special' ice cream to mark Chesterfield's great footballing achievement when the local team made it to the semi-finals of the FA cup back in 1997.

In 1999 the firm acquired Thimble Hall, in Youlgreave, and in collaboration with the Peak National Park Authority Bruno's son, John, has now perfected the latest environmentally friendly ice-cream to be sold under the Thimble Hall name. The ice-cream will be made using Frederick's expertise, using high quality organic ingredients from the Peak District and will be sold through selected outlets including Thimble Hall. The one-up one-down Grade II listed cottage has been used as an antique shop and cobblers but never before as an ice cream parlour!

The company celebrated the millennium in its own way, updating its mobile operation using the newest Ford Transit vans which are professionally coach built and fitted with the very best technical equipment to ensure that the public will receive their original 1898 blend ice-cream packed cones and wafers in the very best condition.

Top: *The original mid-Victorian horse-drawn ice-cream cart from 1873, made and used by the first generation of Fredericks in the ice-cream trade.*
Above: *Bruno Frederick outside Thimble Hall.*
Left: *One of the current ice-cream vans in today's fleet selling both soft and scooped ice-cream, stored under the most hygienic conditions even for today's stringent conditions.*

Above: Generations of Chesterfield people have found employment at Robinsons. In 1965 the company's workforce numbered 3,752, and here we see the printing department engaged upon its daily work in that same year. Letterpress printing began at the company's Holme Brook works in 1892, and litho printing was introduced in 1901. Working conditions and machinery changed over the years, but one thing that never altered was the company's caring attitude towards its employees and their welfare. In return, workers were expected to be loyal and committed. One illustration of the ethos which prevailed was the importance which was placed on good time-keeping. During the 1920s workers could earn themselves a silver or gold badge to be worn on the collar; the silver badge was given when they had completed five years' service without ever being late. At that time workers were required to wear an overall which was provided by the company but which they had to pay for; most of them chose to do this by having a few pence deducted from their pay packet each week. The overalls of the 1920s were of course very different from the plain, practical overalls, with the company logo sewn onto the pocket, seen in this photograph.

Below centre: Here we see the 'Steelbreaking & Dismantling Co' busy dismantling a lamp post in Chesterfield. The circumstances are not known, but the date is given as the 1950s, and the casual workclothes of those doing the dismantling remind us that this was an era when we were all far less safety-conscious. We drove around without seatbelts, we rode motorcycles with the wind in our hair, and apparently we also dismantled lamp posts quite cheerfully with no hard hats, even though there was a large hook swinging about above our heads that looked quite heavy enough to crack our skulls open. The Trades Union movement rose to prominence in the post-war years and is often remembered chiefly for its efforts to secure better wages for workers, but another very significant achievement was in fostering a culture where bosses and workers alike recognised the importance of instigating proper safety precautions in the workplace. In many cases this involved adopting safer working practices, issuing protective clothing, and providing formal training and proper supervision. We suspect that a 21st century works inspector would be horrified by the antics of these chaps - working at the roadside with no reflective clothing, no protective headgear, perhaps even no steel-capped boots - but at that time nobody would have given it a second thought.

Providing education for the community

North Derbyshire Tertiary College was formed in 1931 as the Clowne Mining and Technical Institute, built on a grant of £6,000 from the Miners Welfare Commission. The original building had only four rooms - two laboratories, a drawing office and a classroom. A series of extensions have developed it into a large, modern Further Education College.

Clowne Campus is now just one of ten other centres offering further education under the umbrella of North Derbyshire Tertiary College. The Campus aims to meet the training and educational needs of it's local community, this is principally the Bolsover District and the North East Derbyshire areas which border on to South Yorkshire. The main difference between Clowne and the other sites is that an important dimension of its work is with 14 - 19 year olds, from school link programmes to the Heritage sixth form centre.

The provision on Campus has radically changed since the decline of the coal industry and has entered the 21st Century meeting a diverse range of learning needs. It incorporates young people and adults with learning difficulties and disabilities along with employed adults who wish to improve their professional skills.

Mining technology and subsidiary occupations have now been replaced by courses in Information Technology, for example, Computing Business and Office Technology. Vocational training includes holistic therapy, beauty therapy and hairdressing; it provides both school leavers and adults with the skills needed to embark upon a successful career.

Another important development has been the introduction of full-time courses for adults aiming to progress on to Higher Education. This has proved very popular with adults in the area who wish to retrain and, to date, has enabled over 200 people to enter University or other Colleges for HND and Degree courses. The Campus has further developed this provision by offering a GEMS (General Education for Mature Students) course.

North Derbyshire Tertiary College has witnessed a great many changes since opening in 1931. However, the biggest and most important factor has been the development and transformation of culture at the College. Open access, social inclusion and flexibility are the ideas behind a philosophy that gives the Campus a Community College ethos.

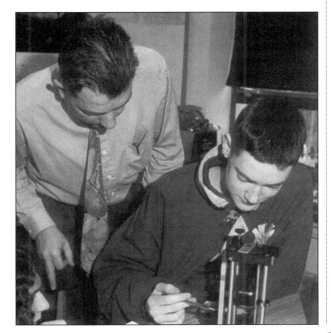

Above: The new main entrance of the North Derbyshire Tertiary College. Far left: Students studying for A levels in the Heritage Sixth Form Centre. Left: The comprehensive, well equipped library is available to all full and part-time students.

From horses to e-commerce

The idea of hiring rather than buying ones means of transport must be as old as transport itself. No doubt within a short time of the first man, having tamed the first wild horse, he was offering to hire out its services to someone else. Today, of course, when we talk about vehicle hire we usually mean hiring a car.

On 8th February 2000 the entire share capital of one of Chesterfield's longest established businesses, Kenning Car Van & Truck Rental, was acquired by Sixt AG the market leading German vehicle rental company. The new Sixt Kenning produced a combined vehicle rental organisation comprising a

Above: *Frank Kenning, founder of the Kenning empire, opened a hardware business in Clay Cross.*
Right: *George Kenning collected thousands of Queen's Honey Soap Coupons to purchase the first Kenning car.* *Below:* *Frank Kenning (jnr) with a young helper, circa 1900, promoting the Kenning hardware business.*

European network and representation in the USA, a total fleet of more than 90,000 vehicles and the convenience of more than 1,000 rental locations, including full facilities at international and regional airports.

The Kenning business traces its roots back to the late 19th century when Frank Kenning opened a hardware business in Clay Cross selling a variety of goods including glass, china, candles, kerosene and petrol - products which soon resulted in a progression to involvement with the fledgling motor trade. At the turn of the century the sale of petroleum products developed into a distribution business for petroleum products throughout Derbyshire using horse drawn petrol tankers. At the time the firm was able to reach an historic distribution agreement between it and Consolidated Petroleum Ltd - a forerunner of Shell and BP. Needless to say Frank Kenning's interest in the internal combustion engine soon led the firm to switch from using horse drawn petrol tankers: his dozen horses and their equipment were sold in 1910 as result of the purchase of a motor lorry and car.

George, later Sir George Kenning, Frank's son, followed his father as head of the business and

QUEEN'S HONEY
SOAP COUPONS.

THOUSANDS WANTED.
2¼d. per Dozen Given in Cash or Goods.
Apply—

F. KENNING & SONS,
CLAY CROSS.

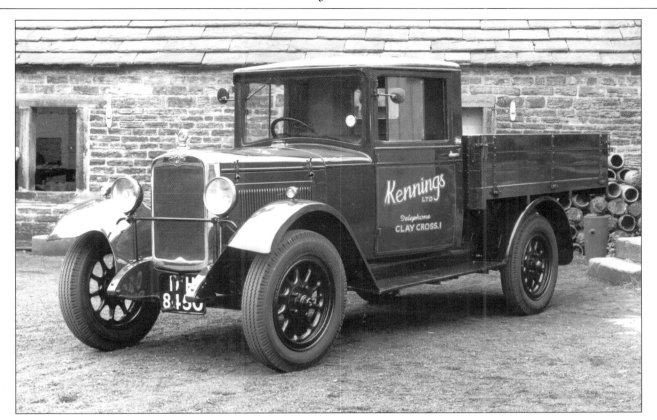

quickly saw the opportunities in the growing motor car market. In 1915 George obtained a Ford franchise for the firm, now called Frank Kenning and Sons. That franchise was followed later by a distributorship for Morris cars in Derbyshire. The first ever fleet order for Morris cars was placed by Kennings when it bought 181 two seater Morris cars for the Shell-Mex organisation. One of Sir George's largest deals came in 1927 when he bought the entire Morris factory's surplus production for £62,925. In 1938 the firm became a public company, Kennings Ltd. Subsequent mergers, acquisitions and developments saw Kennings gaining franchises for Austin, Morris, NIG, Standard, Triumph, Rover and Daimler cars.

Following the end of the second world war growth was massive. By 1950 the firm had 50 depots and by the time of Sir George Kenning's death in 1956 there were 80. Sir George was followed by his son, another George, as Chairman. George Kenning junior and his brother David became joint managing directors.

The Kenning brothers dedicated themselves to expanding the Kenning Motor Group as it had by then become. Soon the firm had grown to 300 depots with interests in motor vehicles, fuel, car and van rental and tyres and had over 8,000 employees.

Perhaps the most notable acquisition was the London Rolls Royce and Austin distributor, Car Mart, which held the Royal Warrant to supply HM the Queen with vehicles along with a BMC import and distributorship operation in Southern Rhodesia, now Zimbabwe. The acquisition of Car Mart made Kennings the world's largest distributor of Austin cars.

The Kenning group expanded horizontally moving outwards from motor sales: the Kenning Tyres Services business, for example, was developed into a national network becoming one of the largest suppliers of tyres for cars, commercial vehicles and earth movers as well as operating three remould factories and marketing its own label Fisk and John Bull tyre brands. The Kennings tyre business began in 1934 when Tyresoles Ltd appointed Kennings the concession making it the first independent tyre remoulder appointed to use the Tyresoles remoulding process. Eventually Kennings would have not only its remould factories but also over 95 Kenning Tyre Service depots.

Top: A Kenning Morris Commercial - one of the many Austins that Kenning sold or hired for purchase in the 1930s. Above: Sir George Kenning was the first of the Kenning family to expand the business into the motor car trade.

The most well known of the Kenning companies however was the Kenning car and van rental business. Kennings were early entrants to the rental business: soon after the turn of the last century horses were regularly hired to BP - as well as bicycles to Shell amongst many other customers. In fact the real entry to self drive hire came much later when Kennings purchased Self Motoring Ltd the British pioneers of car hire.

Self Motoring Ltd was acquired by Kennings only in 1954 and specialised in short term vehicle hire. The hire business grew even larger with the acquisition of the Irish company Joe Malone Car Hire along with the purchase of a similar business in France. By 1970 the company had a hire fleet of 5,000 vehicles.

In an echo of the early petrol sales by its founder the company also operated more than 100 petrol stations selling more than 33 million gallons of petrol each year. The Kenning group built the motorway services on the M5 at Strensham and at Anderton on the M61 whilst also operating a distribution company for Shell-Mex and BP.

The company even expanded into driving schools, operating from over 40 centres with approved instructors teaching pupils in late model cars fitted with dual controls. And of course car drivers need insurance - a need Kennings was quick to meet with Kenning Insurance Brokers with 15 offices having access to most of the major insurance companies and offering advice and competitive rates for all types of insurance.

Another substantial side of the business was vehicle building with factories producing the famous three wheel W&E electric milk float in Shrewsbury and road tankers at Ossett in West Yorkshire, where Kenning Road Tankers assembled complete tankers for the carriage of oils, spirits and chemicals including many for the largest oil companies and their authorised distributors.

George Kenning junior died in 1981 followed by his brother David in 1982. The brothers were succeeded by Bart Oxspring and Jerry Foster. Four years later however the Kenning Motor Group was taken over by Tozer, Kemsley and Millbourn.

As a result of the take-over the Kennings Group was split up and the majority of its assets disposed of, though many of its vehicle distributorships and franchises were merged with another TKM company, Wadham Stringer, to become Wadham Kenning.

In 1992 the Inchcape Group acquired Tozer Kemsley and Millbourn. Two years later a new company was

Top: *A line-up of Kenning hire vehicles in the late 1970s.* ***Above:*** *Subtle changes to the Kenning livery in the early 1980s.* ***Left:*** *A Kenning vehicle from 1990.*

formed incorporating the interests of both Kenning Car and Van Rental together with the United Rental Group to form the United Kenning Rental Group.

The new group would be the largest vehicle rental company in the UK with its 82 offices, 11,000 vehicles from Kenning Car & Van Rental: combined with licensees of United Rental System they now had 175 outlets and 13,000 vehicles.

Today the company hires cars, vans, trucks and minibuses to corporate fleet markets, private individuals and business travellers, whilst abroad the company not only rents vehicles but also is involved in selling second hand cars, car leasing and even has a travel agency. Main customers in the UK include all major leasing companies, the Post Office, Government departments, major construction and utility companies and local authorities. The business has many alliances with major hotel companies and airlines

Uniquely the company is the only UK rental company to have both a substantial car and light commercial vehicle fleet - most rental companies specialising in either one or the other.

Whilst proud of having a remarkable history the firm looks constantly to the future: advanced technology allows vehicle reservations to be made via the internet whilst technology also allows the use of WAP phones, car express machines, on-line car auctions and fleet

management. 'E-Sixt' the company's internet service enables on-line booking within a few seconds and on-line fleet control - the first internet fleet control management system ever devised. The system provides a wide range of on-line leasing offers, many thousands of used cars, a comfortable solution for professional fleet management for corporate clients as well as a vast amount of data about scheduled airline flights world-wide.

The company is confident that E-Sixt is going to provide the main platform for future business growth offering the customer convenience, efficiency and outstanding service.

The tiny business started by Frank Kenning in the late 19th century has certainly changed over the years!

Top left: Most recently, Kenning Car Van & Truck Rental has expanded its fleet by buying 500 new Ford Iveco vans. Top right: A Kenning transit in the mid 1990s. Above right: The new face of Sixt Kenning. Right: Sixt Kenning now has its office in Durrant House, the former site of Chesterfield's Royal Hospital (built 1859), where it continues as one of the UK's largest car and van rental businesses and one of Chesterfield's largest employers.

No watering down of standards

A man who developed a feel for the land while he worked as a farmer was able to turn this to good advantage when, having had a new bungalow built in 1950, he found the water supply available was inadequate. Presented with this very practical problem, Richard 'Dick' Marriott started to study rock formations and water sources. Soon he was out on the local hills around his Spitewater Farm, Stonedge, Ashover with dowsing sticks and was able to locate a water source. Trusting his judgement he started drilling and found his own domestic water supply. That was back in the 1940s and the hole he bored then is still servicing the bungalow as well as two local pubs, a Methodist Chapel and two cottages. He had previously been helping other local farmers with their machinery and had gained the trust and respect by his skill in repairing faulty engines, fabricating parts if necessary and being prepared to work through the night so that vital farming equipment was out of action for as short a time as possible during the difficult days of the second world war.

This was the time when there was enormous pressure on farmers to increase food production and as improvements to farm machinery came and the acreage of farms increased along with stock levels, the demand for water also became greater. Dick was quick to appreciate the implications of this and he designed his first drilling rig, a free-standing tripod. This was followed by a drill which had a mast and pneumatic action - he purchased the lorry with the chassis then fabricated all the associated equipment including the hydraulics. This rig drilled over 150 holes. This was to set a pattern of him developing the tools necessary to carry out his specialised trade, a skill inherited by his grandsons. This skill has ensured that the Marriott family firm is among the top operators in the country.

Over time the willow dowsing twigs were replaced with whalebones tipped with copper. Water divining involves holding the V-shaped whalebone tightly against the chest and striding out across the place where water is sought. When over an underground water source, the stick jerks earthwards. Apparently most people can get this far but the real skill is in estimating accurately how much water and at what depth it is to be found. Dick Marriott had these skills developed to a high degree, Paul also possesses this

Top left: *Company founder Richard (Dick) Marriott.*
Above: *A wheeled rig used in the 1950s.*
Below: *Working on an early site in the 1950s.*

skill, he maintains that it requires a life-time of practice to develop maximum accuracy. So confident did Dick become in his ability to find underground water that he would often undertake commissions on a 'no water, no fee' basis and it was his proud boast that he never drilled a dry well. Up to the time of his death, in 1987, he had drilled over 2,000 holes in England and Wales and that is no small achievement. Even with all this success in the family there is still no clear under-standing of how dowsing actually works, Dick had a theory that it was to do with electricity but all they know for sure is that it gets results.

An example of his expertise which proved the findings of scientific surveys inaccurate is found in the case of a request from Northampton. The geologist's report said there was no water below 70 feet. Dick insisted there was water at 240 feet and a supply of around 3,500- 4,000 gallons an hour. The results of pump

testing resulted in a yield of 4,000 gallons an hour at a pumped level of 242 feet.

He was called in to solve the problems of the drought-hit Derbyshire village of Youlgreave. The local water committee had failed to discover what they felt sure was a leak in the mains taking water from the spring where the villagers drew their water. Despite heavy rainfalls the spring level remained low and 15 houses were suffering a serious water shortage. The family wash had to be done in the late evening and baths had to be taken at the time of lowest water consumption - midnight. The water committee, probably the smallest water company in the country at the time having only 1,000 customers, decided to call in Dick Marriott to save digging up the main street in search of a leak. This was a hard case as even Dick was temporarily baffled after he'd conducted his first search, high winds prevented the dowsing sticks operating successfully. He returned a week later when condi-tions were more favourable and found the leak, which was cured and has remained satisfactory ever since.

His interests extended beyond water sourcing and well-drilling, however and he was actively involved in the

Above: This revolutionery bit was designed and patented by Dick in the 1970s and is still marketed worldwide today. Left: Paul Marriott, far left, with one of their drilling rigs being used for research and development with Numa Tool Company, USA. Below: Marriott's custom designed casing retrieval system, has a pull back capacity in excess of 800 tons and is capable of retrieving large diameter temporary casing at depths of up to 150 metres.

local brass band scene. He was a founder member and for fourteen years a driving force of the Ashover Brass Band, he even taught himself to play bass. Later he re-formed the Darley Dale Band and launched the first-ever Tansley Band. Representatives of no fewer than eleven brass bands played his favourite hymns at his funeral service.

Dick's aptitude for producing machinery for particular applications continued and in the late 1970s he designed and patented a drilling tool which could simultaneously drill the bore and put the casing in place which prevented the hole collapsing and falling in on itself. This revolutionised the practice of well-boring and the bit is still marketed world-wide, and has formed the base from which other companies have developed their own drilling and casing tools. Later on Dick's grandsons, Paul, Alan and Jonathan patented their design of a machine which could retrieve casings already in the ground with a pull-back capacity of 800 tons from a depth of up to 150 metres. This is the only one of its kind and was developed, just as Dick's original rig was, to meet the requirements of their customers. The company has also co-operated with an American company in its design of a down-hole hammer. A recent addition to the Marriott range of specialist equipment is a series of submersible borehole pumps capable of continuous operation which are suitable for use in deep mine de-watering, reservoir supplies, irrigation, domestic water supply and livestock watering plant applications. A pump for use in larger boreholes can be used for large scale irrigation projects as well as fire-fighting.

Their scope of work extends throughout England, Scotland, Wales and Ireland. The UK's seven major water authorities have benefited from Marriott's services drilling boreholes for public and industrial supply at diameters of up to 42". Contracts have been carried out in Northern Ireland for Coca Cola Bass Brewery and other large drinks consumers. Marriott's also have carried out extensive work in the Republic of Ireland on projects for large watering schemes down to spring water bottling companies; the world famous Ballygowan Spring Water comes from two deep boreholes that Marriott's have drilled. In recent years their expertise is being sought in some of the most arrid and remote corners of the world where water is a precious commodity, all stemming from the early days of their Grandfather's beginnings in the 1940s. The environmental impact of well-boring is also addressed and the company seeks not only to minimise damage by adhering to guidelines produced by the Environment Agency and other regulatory bodies but can also provide advice on

Top right: Paul and Alan Marriott. Left: A Pilot Bit, designed and manufactured by Marriotts.

whether an environmental hazard is threatened by pollution from petrol stations and chemical plants, by taking core samples of earth and rock from nearby and submitting them for detailed analysis.

The company's strengths include their innovations in the equipment they offer as well as customer satisfaction and value for money. They also pride themselves on the care with which they maintain their equipment. They recently modified in-house, a new drilling rig and ancillary equipment to enable them to diversify into the on-shore oil and gas industry. The company offers the full range of services to groundwater, oil and gas exploration companies, including drilling and hydrogeo-logical consultancy, and over the years a formi-dable range of expertise has been developed as a result of responding to their customers needs.

The company also offers drilling into abandoned mine workings for the abstraction of methane gas and due to the advanced technology in directional drilling, they are able to steer into old mine

roadways, hitting targets of less than three metres wide in excess of 3,000 feet deep.

After fifty years in their original premises PR Marriott Drilling moved to their present location called, appropri-ately, Springwater House, Danesmoor, near Clay Cross, Chesterfield in 1998.

Building up the company to its present standing has required immense commitment from family members and the firm's employees, involving working long hours and often through inhospitable weather conditions. Operations are now under the direction of the third generation of Marriotts, since Paul, the grandson of the founder of the family business took over as Managing Director, his wife Julie, his two brothers Alan and Jonathan, his mother, Wendy and their loyal employees all have their own individual but considerable input to the company - the business has always been a joint venture.

Above: *Current family members active in the firm are Jonathan, Paul and Alan Marriott.* **Top:** *A recent project drilling for gas in Wales.*

Building on the past

The concept of a mortgage is an old one. Today in Britain the first place one thinks of to obtain a loan to buy a house is a building society. The idea of building societies grew in the middle of the 19th century. Originally a building society would be formed, temporarily, by small groups of people for a single purpose. For example one may have been formed to provide funding for a row of houses or a small estate and would terminate on the completion of the project. Ten people might each want to buy a house. The group would then form a building society into which all would regularly contribute a fixed sum; when enough had been saved to pay for one house the society would instruct a builder to start work. Typically which member got to

occupy each house would be chosen by lot. Ten names went into a bag and the name of the winner drawn out. The winner would then move into his new house and continue making payments to the society until the loan was paid off. As soon as enough money was saved to build a second house another name would be chosen and the process repeated - the second winner would then move in and so on until the last member moved into the last house. When all the houses had been built and paid for such societies would then be wound up.

Above: Charles Binns JP, one of the businessmen who founded Clay Cross Building Society. Above right: Mrs Pendleton's house and White Corn Stores on Thanet Street, Clay Cross. Right: Houses prior to demolition on Eyre Street, the site of the Society's present head office. Below: Clay Cross Building Society's head office.

between Sheffield and London. By the middle of the 20th century the building society was based in the front room of the Secretary's house in Thanet Street. This was the home of Mrs Pendleton who is still remembered; few however are old enough to recall the days when she drove a pony and trap round the surrounding villages collecting subscriptions and dealing with savings accounts and other aspects of the Society's business In 1960 the Society moved next door to number 42 Thanet Street, previously White's Corn Stores, which the Society converted into modern offices with counters in 1968 when Derek Hawley became the Society's manager. In 1992 it moved to its current offices in Eyre Street, a building which had until then been the medical centre but which became available when the GPs moved to new purpose built premises in Eldon Street.

In 1968 when Derek Hawley became manager the Society's assets were less than £1 million, by the time of his retirement they had grown to over £10 million. Mike McDermott who has been manager since 1991 has seen assets double since then.

Assets currently exceed £20 million but the Society continues to operate with just one branch office which serves around 4,000 investors and 550 borrowers, and one agency office in Sutton-in-Ashfield.

Some building societies however would carry on with new members and a new set of houses and these were known as 'permanent' building societies.

Permanent societies provided continuity and also offered a savings and loans services to a wider clientele.

The Clay Cross Building Society, a permanent building society from the outset, was founded in August 1859 as the Clay Cross Benefit Building Society. Appropriately the Society's corporate seal was squares and a compass representing building and construction tools. The new building society was established by a group of local businessmen to serve the local community; the most prominent member of the group was Charles Binns JP, founder of local schools. Charles Binns was Secretary of the Clay Cross Iron & Coal Mining Company, a company which had been formed by George Stephenson to exploit the rich deposits of coal and iron he had discovered whilst tunnelling under the town to complete the main railway line

The Clay Cross Building Society prides itself in offering a friendly, personal and efficient service. As a small independent mutual building society, owned by its members and run for their long term benefit, the Society's principal objectives are to provide savings and mortgage products which offer excellent value for its members maintaining traditional values of integrity and trustworthiness.

Today the Society retains its traditional links with the local community through major sponsorship of the Ashover show plus sponsorship of several smaller shows and societies as well as giving support to local sports teams and schools.

Top: *The Society's agent's office in Sutton-in-Ashfield.*
Above left: *The interior of the head office.*
Right: *Mike McDermott, General Manager.*

More than just boys into men

Mount St Mary's College can trace its educational roots back to the 17th century. Its present form, however, owes much to the vision of Father Randal Lythgoe. He was a member of the Society of Jesus that everyone knows as the Jesuits. The Society's founder, Ignatius Loyola, is famous for his promise, 'Give me the boy and I will give you back the man.' His perception of education was one that spanned the centuries. Children were taken into the care of the Jesuits and were given more than an academic grounding. They received moral and social guidance that equipped them to be valuable members of society. That ethic rings just as true today as it ever did. But, in the 21st century, Loyola's statement can be applied to girls as well as boys. It could now be adapted to say, 'Give me the child and I will give you back the adult.'

*Above: The statue of Our Lady of the Mount erected in the 1880s. **Right**: The old College pictured in 1882. **Below**: The swimming pool, opened in 1916. **Inset**: Boys excavating the swimming pool.*

When Father Lythgoe founded the college on 17 September 1842 his intentions were clear. Originally known as Spinkhill College, the school set out to provide educational opportunities that were within the financial reach of large families with limited incomes. Just 30 pupils walked through the portals on the first day, but the college's reputation spread rapidly. By 1865 there were 120 new entrants ready to take their place at The Mount. Space was severely restricted as the facilities were still geared up to accommodate just the original intake numbers. The College was bursting at the seams, a victim of its own success. Many a prayer was said to the statue of Our Lady of the Mount for her intercession in helping alleviate the difficulties. Potential entrants were turned away throughout the 1870s and 1880s until

resources for physical education and recreation. Educational and social excursions are arranged to make sure that the widest possible experiences are on offer. The environment is both a safe and attractive backdrop to the learning process.

The school is rich in its own history and is rightly proud of the nostalgia it evokes. It is fiercely proud of its dedication to the Virgin Mary, Our Lady Immaculate and is rightly proud that it has provided 360 Jesuit priests for the English province. As the new millennium unfolds The Mount is ready to meet the demands and challenges that the future will bring. A modern ICT suite is already in place, created out of what were old classrooms. The college has entirely refitted and refurbished the old theatre and the magnificently equipped and furnished leisure centre was opened in 1998. An attractively laid out music room opened towards the end of 2000. All this attention to modern demands shows that Mount St Mary's has been able to blend the traditional with the current, without ever losing sight of the educational ideals of Saint Ignatius Loyola. One of the houses, once known as Rhetoric House, now bears the Founder's name. He would be proud to know that through its doors he is now giving back to the world not just men, as he once promised, but citizens of both sexes.

sufficient funds could be raised to erect extension buildings to the old red stone of Middleton Hall, the original building. Further adaptations have taken place over the last century to ensure that the pressure on Mount St Mary's has never again returned to such proportions.

Tony Blair, the leader of the Labour party in the 1997 general election, was helped past the winning post with his slogan of 'Education, education, education'. The Society of Jesus had been issuing the same message for centuries beforehand. Mount St Mary's had also offered more than just the traditional three Rs. Even in its earliest days it provided a broad curriculum. As the years rolled by it made adaptations as society's needs and expectations changed. The parents of the student boarders are confident in the knowledge that their children are receiving a rich and varied learning base in a unit that is just as much a family as the one at home. There is a feeder preparatory school at Barlborough and the links with The Mount provide the opportunity for children, whether day pupils or boarders, to have a balanced and continuous education right through to the age of 18. There are strong traditions of music and drama that offer children with individual artistic gifts the chance to nurture those talents. The well equipped gymnasium and attractive swimming pool are well used

Top left: *An aerial view of Mount St Mary's College taken in the 1930s.* ***Above left:*** *The front of the old College pictured in 1992.* ***Right:*** *Charles Harrison holds the Daily Mail Cup after victory at Twickenham in 1994.* ***Below:*** *A recent view of Loyola House.*

Frank Smith - caring for the customer

In 1945 Frank Smith left William Rhodes School and started as a radio apprentice at the long established Chesterfield's Murphy dealer of Roy Smith, (incidentally, no relation of Frank's), in Cavendish Street. In those early days Frank attended Chesterfield Technical College for three nights a week and a whole day, (thanks to the generosity of Roy Smith), to gain as much knowledge as possible to progress his chosen career.

After serving two years National Service in the RAF as a Radar Technician, he returned to complete his apprenticeship with Roy Smith. Television started in the early 1950s and Frank's experience with Radar stood him in good stead to progress in this new technology. In 1958 this led Frank to start his own business in Bolsover and in 1963 the limited company of F L Smith (Electrical) was formed. The industry then entered a period of innovation with the steady growth of new technology such as Colour Television, Video recorders, Satellite TV, Automatic Washing machines, Fridge-Freezers and many others.

In 1971 a branch was opened in Shirebrook which was expanded a year later. The Chesterfield shop opened in 1974 and moved to its present location in Knifesmithgate three years later. In 1985, a fourth shop was opened in Regent Street, Mansfield with a fifth branch in Bridge Place, Worksop being established in 1991. In 1993 the Company took over the Roy Smith company and continued to trade from its Cavendish Street branch until it's lease expired in 1999. This was a poignant moment for Frank Smith because it meant he had gone full circle during his working life.

Although Frank Smith has never changed the basic philosophy of his business, a philosophy that other members of his family now share, he has moved with the times. Customers are not only getting top quality service, Frank Smith ensures his prices remain keen with buying power through the firm's membership of CI Holdings, the largest buying group in the country, which is now affiliated to 'EURONICS' throughout Europe. They are also members of The Radio, Television and Electrical

Top: *Frank Smith's Mansfield store.*
Above: *The Bolsover shop.* ***Left:*** *Chesterfield's Frank Smith store.*

Retailers Association and adhere to their Code of Practice. The Company has been a member of RETRA since 1970 and Mr Smith was its President in 1992 and 1993.

Testament to the success of the business is its longevity, as Mr Smith explains, 'because we have been in the business for forty-three years it means we are here to stay.' This means that every customer they deal with knows the Company is backed by immense experience both in the products they sell or rent and in the after sales service.

Today Mr Smith's family runs the company with Gary Hurst the Sales Director, Nigel Cowley the Finance Director and both Mr Smith's daughters are Directors. This means that the Company will continue to be with the people of Chesterfield for a long time to come. It has a staff of 30, some of whom have been with the Company for more than 25 years.

The Company has always been proud of its honesty - there are no hidden extras for the customers to find. At the end of the day the customer wins on all counts, whether it is the quality of the goods that the firm sells or rents, the quality of it's service, or the competitiveness of it's prices.

Although there have been many changes in product technology and business legislation, over the years many companies in the same profession have fallen by the wayside, the market place being a poorer place for their disappearance. Events like these have made the Company more professional in the way it chooses products and presents itself to customers - commitment to their needs being of paramount importance.

The size of the Company means it is able to quickly change direction to keep in step with today's changing market. Customers get the benefit of all the latest trends in technology backed up by a service that only an independent retailer can give.

Frank Smith is very proud of their unique philosophy compared to other Electrical outlets. From the day a customer buys or rents a product the Company looks after it. The Company has it's own in-house Service Department with fully trained engineers who play a major part in the Customer Care After Sales policy.

Frank Smith Home Electric Centres owe their success to traditional values, making all their customers feel special and cared for. This gives the Company an edge in today's marketplace and secures a long and prosperous future.

Top right: *The shop in Worksop.* ***Above left:*** *A hi-tech television display in the Worksop branch.* ***Left:*** *White goods on display in the Chesterfield store.*

Music to the ears of Chesterfield

Boy bands come and boy bands go. Ragtime has been replaced by rap. Video stands in the market place where radio valves once flickered and whirred. For a century CE Hudson has seen it all come and go. The firm will still be providing the same efficient and well informed service to customers when their tastes and styles have moved on to whatever developments this century brings.

John Galsworthy was writing 'The Forsyte Saga' and music hall artists were all the rage in 1906 when Charles Edward Hudson left his employment in the piano department of J White and Son. He helped set up the partnership of Catts and Hudson in Commercial Yard, selling pianos, organs and other musical instruments. In those Edwardian days most middle class homes had a piano and musical get togethers for the whole family was a feature of British life. Its equivalent today is probably a set of couch potatoes slumped in front of the box.

Thankfully, there are still enough of us left who enjoy making music to keep this part of Hudson's trade flourishing.

The founder did not keep his partner for long; within 12 months Mr Catts was off to try pastures new and emigrated to New Zealand. Charles Hudson bought his share and ploughed his lone, but successful, furrow. Mr Hudson had a keen business sense and marketed his goods at an attractive price as he built up his client base. One

of his best selling items was the violin on sale for 4s 9d (24p). There has been some resistance from the present management to restoring the old price ticket to current stock! Although the early days went well the company nearly went under during the 1914-18 war. Charles Hudson was away on active service and the war effort left people with little money or initiative to spare in the pursuit of musical instruments. On his return from serving king and country the founder built up the sales of pianos and organs as these were still at the heart of music in the home.

Stanley Hudson joined the firm in 1929. He had spent his formative years in the trade working for Danemann & Co, the London piano manufacturers. His excellent grounding there was of great benefit to Hudson's, but, once again, development was inhibited by gunfire. Stanley Hudson served in the armed forces when the balloon went up in 1939. The

Above: *Company founder CE Hudson.*
Left:*Catts & Hudson's very first catalogue compiled in 1906.*

lone, but successful, furrow. Mr Hudson had a keen business sense and marketed his goods at an attractive price as he built up his client base. One

growth of Hudson's had been put on hold, but was able to take off again on his return.

As well as selling musical instruments, Hudson's has always been receptive to the developments in recorded music. When Charles Hudson began his partnership the shop was so up to date that it sold phonograph records. The huge boom in sales of records after World War II and the massive demand for 45s when they came out in the late 1950s did not take Hudson's by surprise. It already had

half a century of experience on which to draw. Hudson's became a limited company in 1956, with Stanley as the managing director, a position he held until 1994. Keith Hudson, the current MD, joined the family firm when Elvis Presley was first entering the hit parade and Jimmy Young was still headlining concerts.

Camilla Hudson, the director of the video department, is the fourth generation of Hudsons to be involved in the company that is known as 'the musical centre'.

It first occupied premises in the Market Hall in 1935 and, when larger premises were needed, moved some of its business to the NatWest building in 1969. The shop on the outer side of Market Hall was kept until 1976, but the separate outlet inside the hall is still going strong. This has kept a link with the building that goes right back to 1906 as Catts and Hudson used to trade from the Market Hall on Saturdays, in addition to their premises in Commercial Yard.

The current premises in the NatWest building underwent alterations in 1996 and is now able to offer a comprehensive range of musical business. Schoolchildren buy their recorders alongside rock musicians purchasing synthesisers. CDs, DVDs, tapes and videos are all there for every taste. Whether you want to try to be the next violinist to follow in Vanessa Mae's footsteps or merely wish to listen to Rolf Harris crucify a rock classic, then CE Hudson will serve you well.

Above: More pages from Catts & Hudson's very first catalogue compiled in 1906.
Left: A Phillips chart list from August 1955.

Working the land for over 40 years

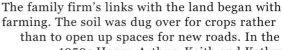

Ruttle Plant (Midlands) Ltd is based at Holmewood. From this nerve centre the company handles plant hire and excavation work for the construction industry. The firm is part of the Ruttle Group that includes Ruttle Plant Hire Ltd and it has become established as a major force nationally, largely thanks to the drive and initiative of positive management. The distinctive purple dipper arms and R logo on the earth moving equipment have long been a common sight across the Midlands and are now being seen more and more further afield.

The family firm's links with the land began with farming. The soil was dug over for crops rather than to open up spaces for new roads. In the 1950s Harry, Arthur, Keith and Kathryn Ruttle lived on their parents' farm. Mr and Mrs GH Ruttle formed the company, Ruttle Plant Hire, in 1956. Harry drove the first machine that they owned. His brothers and sister were still finishing off school and they continued in daytime education and helped their parents out on the farm in the evenings. Harry helped keep the infant business afloat until his brothers and sister were ready to join him in building it up towards the position of significance it holds today. The first piece of machinery they owned was a Massey Ferguson backhoe loader. By the mid 1990s the Ruttle Group had snowballed to a company with a £40 million annual turnover. Virtually every form of construction equipment and aspect of contractors' plant now comes under its remit.

The company was founded in Leyland, Lancashire and operated from there for several years. The headquarters then made the short journey to Blackburn Street, Chorley before moving again in 1980 to Lancaster House, Ackhurst Road, Chorley. These were purpose built premises that enabled Ruttle's to rationalise and maximise the business. The move to Chesterfield followed as business boomed. To date there have been three generations of the family running the firm, balancing profit with giving an efficient and reliable service in a notoriously cut throat sector. That it not just survived but thrived is a

This page: *Various items of plant available from Ruttle Plant (Midlands) Ltd.*

particularly with plant hire and on and off site earth works. The rainbow colours on its lorries have become part and parcel of the accepted Chesterfield scenery. Ruttle's plan to keep it that way and to expand its range of equipment. It has always had a keen eye for

testament to the quality for which Ruttle's has become famous. In 1995 the Ruttle Group made a major decision to take it even further forward. It acquired EW Ambrose of Chesterfield, a bulk earth-works specialist, that also had a small plant hire section. Ruttle's changed the Ambrose emphasis from earth moving to plant hire. However, it did not throw out the baby with the bathwater. Whilst the emphasis might have changed, the earth moving side of the business remained. The Ruttle management intended that, in time, both sides of the operation would experience growth. Ambrose kept its name within the company, though its machines all adopted the Ruttle colour scheme and logo. Eventually, in July 1999, the Ruttle family formed Ruttle Plant (Midlands) Ltd to replace EW Ambrose.

Ruttle Plant is a member of the Road Haulage Association and the Construction Plant Hire Association. It services most of the country's major contractors,

Harry helped keep the business afloat until his brothers and sister were ready to join him

investing in new plant when the time was right. It has never been a company that has rested on its laurels. It has striven to match customer expectations with the service it delivers. The equipment may have changed dramatically since that first Massey Ferguson that Harry drove, but the commitment to doing a good job for an acceptable profit margin has remained the same. The next time you see that unique purple dipper arm, think Ruttle.

This page: More items of plant, including tipper trucks and low loaders, available to hire from Ruttle Plant (Midlands) Ltd.

On the road again

Charles Holland, the founder of Chesterfield's C&J Holland Transport company, was born, one of ten children, in 1927 at Pudding Pie Hill, Wigley. On Saturdays as a boy he would love to rise at 4am to go for journeys in his Uncle Fred's truck. And not content with those adventures Charles would often wait by the roadside at the top of Chandlers Hill, Eastmoor to flag down passing lorry drivers and hitch a lift with them to wherever they were going - the destination didn't matter, the journey was the thing. Later, after leaving school at the age of 13, Charles would eventually spend seven years working as a driver himself for the Boythorpe Haulage company.

Charles' early love of road transport was probably inherited from his father, Alfred, a man who had helped bring the first steam-powered road roller to the area from his native Buckinghamshire. Not even the tragic death of Charles' younger brother Kenneth killed by a truck at the age of 13, could dim Charles fascination with the road.

In 1963 Charles sold his beloved Austin and put the money towards the cost of buying his own 1952 Dodge Diesel for £300. He was soon hauling coal from the 'A' Winning colliery at Blackwell to ICI in Buxton taking five loads a day.

A year later Charles bought a 1942 ex-army Bedford truck from J Hall of Eastmoor. The truck came complete with a council contract and a driver, his uncle Fred with whom Charles had 'ridden shotgun' as a boy. Things soon went wrong however, the Dodge

repeatedly broke down until an exploded differential eventually sealed its doom. After 18 months of struggling, and although the Bedford truck continued to work, Charles gave up driving himself and went back working an excavator for Currall, Lewis and Martin at an open-cast mining site at Mastin Moor.

Meanwhile the Bedford lorry continued to work on the council contract but financial difficulties were soon encountered. The taxman decided the income gained was 'unearned' and declared its intention to apply punitive taxation.

There was however a welcome way out of the tax problem. Killing two birds with one stone Charles Holland was able to not only deal with the taxman but also recognise the enormous input and support he had received from his wife Joan over the years. And so the firm of C&J Holland came into being the 'J' in the title being a timely tribute to Joan Holland. The following year the firm bought a David Brown tractor for £90 and employed Charles' father Alfred to drive it around the Holymoorside area cutting hedges and verges under contract from the council. In 1967 Charles decided to try his luck again and invested £300 in two BMC trucks. A year later he replaced one of the BMCs with a 1958 Seddon bought for £150.

Above: *Early invoices for the purchase of lorries by the company.*
Right: *1965 Riever Albion.*

Yard. An heroic attempt to roll two tyres at once soon resulted in mayhem on the main road.

Space eventually became a problem however so for six months the firm did its parking and servicing in a public car park in Chesterfield town centre, following which it moved to the old fire engine garages at School Board Lane. By then the fleet consisted of seven trucks.

In 1969 a second hand body was fitted to a brand new TK Bedford chassis cab, bought for £1,750 from Blake's on Chatsworth Road. It was used as a snow plough gritter for a council contract.

Two years later a contract was landed at the Avenue Coking Plant, Wingerworth, to remove ashes twice a day, every day of the year. The ashes were transported to Ranskill and Dinnington where they were used to make breeze blocks for the building trade. The Seddon was now replaced by a 1960 Albion Riever costing £600.

At that time internal work at collieries was plentiful so Charles invested in three six-wheel Dodges, buying two of them from Longcliffe Quarries. He also bought two Fodens, one from Arthur Loy of Belper and one from Corkers Transport of Bramton. During those days Charles would act as relief driver often working up to 36 consecutive hours without rest.

Parking and maintenance had been carried out at FA Greaves' premises at Whitebank Yard, Derby Road. The Holland home in Baden Powell Road was a base too. Charles and Joan's second son Andrew distinctly recalls six new lorry tyres being delivered to the family home and himself, at the age of ten, being assigned to roll them, one by one, along Derby Road to Whitbank

Above left: *Charles Holland, the company's founder.*
Above right: *Joan Holland with the Austin that Charles sold to buy his first truck.*

The Avenue Coking Plant contract ended in 1971. At the same time colliery work began to dry up and the firm diversified into hauling stone and aggregates. Another move soon followed first to Kennelly's Plant yard at Winsick, Hasland and later when Kennelly's became a Gypsy caravan site to Clements Yard at Clay Cross. In 1974 however land at Wharf Lane was bought to provide a home for the now reduced fleet of three Riever.

During the next eight years two more Leyland Rievers were bought. The five trucks were used to move coal from the Arkwright colliery to the nearby Coalite plant as well as coal from the Clipstone colliery.

Because of its reliance on colliery work the firm faced serious difficulties during the miners strike of 1984. Charles suffered a heart attack and his HGV licence was taken away. Charles' son Andrew, who then worked for Spire Transport, helped service the trucks at night after he had finished work. Andrew had attended college for six years and not only passed his City and Guilds in technology and engineering but had been proclaimed student of the year by both the Institute of Motor Engineers and the Institute of Road Transport Engineers.

make a success of the business. In 1988 Andrew became partner and David in 1998.

Today David drives a Mercedes six wheel tipper and is the company's representative on the road. Andrew takes care of all maintenance and servicing and, together with Charles, sees to the day the day running of the business helped by Andrew's son Lee.

The company now runs a fleet of 17 trucks. Main customers include Vesuvius UK Ltd, Danisco Pack, Quartex Chemicals, Molloy Freight Forwarding, Amber Plastics, Andrew Hubbuck Transport Services, Tarmac Roadstone, RMC Ltd, Fitzwise, Coe-Crete and Coal Products Ltd. In the past five years the firm has invested half a million pounds in its vehicles, a far cry from that first investment of £300.

By 1986 the company was back on its feet once more with five Leylands carrying coal, stone, sand and Tarmac products. Andrew came to work with his father and Charles youngest son, David, also joined the firm. Recovery necessitated some very hard work with all three men having to go out delivering sacks of concessionary coal to retired miners in a morning to ensure that trucks could be available when needed. Other general haulage work taken on in this period included delivering rubber mats to JCB, ERF, and Foden factories as well as delivering refractory products to foundries and steel works.

And Charles, now 73 years old, and on his third pace maker, still puts in a 12 hour day and is still 'the Boss'.

Above: *Some of the fleet used in the 1980s and 1990s.*
Below: *The latest acquisition, an M.A.N. 26; 284.*

The end of 1986 saw Holland Transport move from Wharf Lane to its present location at Whitting Valley Road, Old Whittington.

Since then Charles, Andrew and David have worked together to

Consideration and Co-operation

The Chesterfield and District Co-op is now more than a century old having reached its centenary as far back as 1994. Co-ops of course go back much further than 1894: even the Chesterfield Co-op was far from being the first such society.

The co-op movement can trace its philosophical origins to the Levellers and Diggers of the 16th century and to other utopian socialist movements which had spontaneously arisen wearing many different guises. The idea of a co-operative store where members could collectively buy goods at wholesale prices seems to have been the idea of a Dutchman, Peter Plockboy, living in London, who in 1659 set out his ideas in a pamphlet describing how a co-op would work - sadly Plockboy's ideas came to nothing at the time.

Clearly however many found the idea of co-operation a lasting inspiration. Some co-operative ventures were started: a co-operative corn mill at Chatham in the 1760s and a tailor's shop in Birmingham in 1777.

In Scotland weavers opened a co-operative store in 1769, whilst the Govan Victualling Society, started in 1777, survived until 1909.

By 1832 there were around 400 co-operative ventures run by 'co-operators' throughout Britain, though the movement towards a national organisation peaked and collapsed in 1835.

The Co-op as we know it today traces its real beginnings to Rochdale in Greater Manchester. The Rochdale Equitable Pioneers' Co-operative Society was established on 15th August 1844 and opened for business on 21st December of that year. The principles and business methods of the Rochdale Co-op quickly led to the formation of other societies along similar successful lines, a situation much helped when co-operatives were granted legal status in 1846.

Above: *The original premises in 1894.*
Below: *The old central premises at West Bars.*

The idea of course was simple, members joined together to buy their goods collectively and thus more cheaply than if they bought them from other retailers - in effect the members became shop owners in their own right.

'Co-operators' were an unusual bunch and as the Co-op movement gathered speed the Co-op took many interesting turns, not least a strong interest in social welfare generally, including adult education and socialist politics.

Premises for the new Chesterfield Co-op were acquired in New Square in March 1894 and the company registered as the Chesterfield and District Co-operative and Provident Society Ltd. The premises opened for business on 28th April.

After six months trading the accounts showed sales of £1,268 and a dividend was declared of one shilling (5p) in the pound to be paid to the Society's then 114 members.

The following year business was growing: a horse and cart were purchased, clothing as well as food began to be sold and the shop moved from New Square to West Bars where ironmongery and drapery were added to the shoppers' choice.

Land was bought in West Bars in 1901 to build new premises which eventually opened in 1903, but not before the first branch Co-op opened at Whittington Moor.

By 1903 the number of members had risen to 1,000, indicative of the interest in and success of the business. So successful was the Co-op that in 1909 it opened a third branch, this time in Brimington, and two years later acquired two more branches when it took over the Whittington Co-op.

On the outbreak of war in 1914 the Co-op's membership had soared to 3,000 and the number of branches had risen to five.

Growth continued despite the problems of operating in a war economy and in 1919 a year after the war's end, a year in which the society became the Chesterfield and District Co-operative Ltd with no fewer than 12 branches, sales for just three months reached

Above centre: *A 1920s reproduction delivery van.*
Below: *A display from 1938.*

be replaced by Dividend Stamps. A whole way of life was ended.

Membership would reach a new record of over 53,000 in 1971 when sales reached £5.6 million: the ten million pound barrier being finally broken in 1976.

For several years membership would decline slightly until new interest was raised in the 1970s and early 1980s when membership would again begin to increase, rising eventually to over 70,000 by 1990.

By the time of the Co-op's centenary sales would have reached more than £33 million annually and membership would stand at almost 75,000.

The Co-op movement and with it the Chesterfield and District Co-operative Society have contributed enormously to the British way of life and to all our memories. Every one of us has shopped at the Co-op, and the older ones amongst us still have vivid memories of the 'divvy'. Can anyone who once had a divvy number ever forget it?

Those 114 members of the Chesterfield Co-op in 1894 no doubt had high hopes for their new enterprise, but even they would have been astonished to see what their baby would grow into.

£60,000. The familiar story of growth continued almost uninterrupted through the 1920s with amalgamation with the Pilsley Society, the opening of more shops, a bakery, the commencement of milk deliveries, an abattoir, the first employees' pension scheme and the creation of a Women's Guild. Such developments were followed in the 1930s by the introduction of a door to door laundry service, selling coal and the building of the Society's new premises at Elder Way. By the outbreak of the second world war annual sales had exceeded £500,000.

Working hours were somewhat reduced as a result of World War II: shops had remained open until 7pm each evening but now the grocery and butchers departments would close on Saturday afternoons. By the war's end 182 members of staff would have served in the forces, whilst sales at the Co-op's 24 stores had reached £625,00 with its now 17,000 members sharing a dividend of £62,000.

It would take only until 1949 for sales to reach the million pound barrier by which time the society had over 20,000 members. In the post war boom sales would increase by over 20 per cent in a single year in 1950 with a dividend declared of 1s 8d in the pound.

By the mid 1960s with 38,000 members turnover would reach over £4 million sharing a typical dividend of 1s 4d in the pound.

The year 1970 saw the end of a great tradition of the Co-op movement - the dividend. The last dividend payment (1s 0d in the pound) was made in that year to

Above left: Central premises in 1944.
Above right: Knifesmithgate in 1994.
Right: Central premises in 1994.

Going, going... but not gone

The year 2000 was a milestone in the history of two long-established Chesterfield estate agencies; two firms which have been serving their clients in Chesterfield and North Derbyshire since the 19th century.

On 1st November 2000 WD Botham & Sons, known as Bothams and founded in 1871, merged with Mitchell and Slaney, a firm founded in the 1890s.

William Drabble Botham, a local butcher, well known to the local farming community, took out an auctioneers licence on 11th July 1872. Trading from Chesterfield's historic Market Hall, William held his first sale of property by public auction outside the Angel Hotel, Chesterfield later that same month. William's son, Joseph Archdale Botham, was taken into partnership around 1890.

Mitchell and Slaney was founded in the 1890s by Ernest Mitchell who practised as a local auctioneer and valuer from Gluman Gate.

Early sales brochures show a wide variety of chattels and property being sold under the hammer of both William Botham and Ernest Mitchell, including herds of pigs, paintings and artefacts - and even the total contents of several factories.

During the 1920s William and Joseph Botham took into partnership Joseph's sons William College and Joseph Archdale junior and from 1925 began trading as WD Botham & Sons. Around that time they also moved to larger premises at Low Pavement.

William College Botham qualified as an Agricultural Auctioneer specialising in agricultural sales and valuations; he played a major role in the development of Chesterfield Cattle Market, with which the firm remained closely associated until its closure during the 1970s.

Following the early death of Joseph Archdale Botham William Botham continued in sole practice throughout the second world war. William took his two sons William Derek and John Knighton Botham, together with John 'Jack' Edward Shemwell, into partnership in 1958.

The inter war period had seen the development of the estate and property side of the Mitchell business as well as auctioneering, with a consequent relocation of the business to larger premises at 73 Saltergate. During the post war period Ernest Mitchell took into partnership Robert Slaney.

By 1959 Robert Slaney purchased the business from the late Ernest Mitchell's estate, taking into partnership his son William Dicken Slaney, and trading as Mitchell & Slaney.

During the following years WD Botham & Sons continued their professional agricultural work, though diversifying in the 1960s in response to the changing property market.

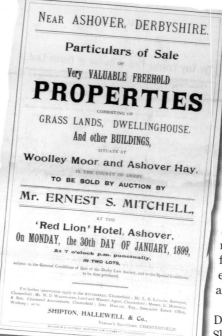

Whilst Derek Botham and Jack Shemwell specialised in agricultural and professional valuation work, in 1971 John Botham began developing the residential property sales side of the business. The firm grew into one of the area's leading independent estate agencies with a fine reputation based upon family traditions, unrivalled experience and integrity.

During the same period Bob Slaney and his son Bill expanded their firm's estate and property management services, eventually building up one of the areas largest managed property portfolios.

In 1975, in advance of Chesterfield's award winning town centre redevelopment scheme, WD Botham & Sons relocated again, this time to purpose built premises at West Bars House, from where the business continues to trade.

Top left: *WD Botham, a local butcher who changed careers to become founder of the oldest independent Estate Agency in Chesterfield.* ***Above:*** *A poster advertising an auction held in 1899, run by Mr Ernest Mitchell.*

The prominent town centre sales office provided an excellent base for marketing a wide range of property together with a full range of valuation services. Around 1982 Bothams would sell the first private residential property in Chesterfield to realise in excess of £100,000. Some 18 years later residential sales would range from properties costing less than £10,000 to those which have sold for more than £1,000,000.

In 1982 Alan James Terry was taken into partnership by Bothams, initially assisting John Botham with increased residential sales and professional valuation work. Subsequently Alan Terry would develop and increase Bothams' commercial and industrial property services which now form a significant part of the firm's business.

During 1990/91 Derek Botham, Jack Shemwell, John Botham and Alan Terry took into partnership Peter Bagnall and Mike Hinch both of whom were born and bred in Chesterfield. The enlarged partnership of experienced Chartered Surveyors and Valuers continued to offer unrivalled local professional experience and knowledge, continuing the established theme of a family partnership which has continually developed and adapted to meet new challenges.

Since the first property sales auction held by William Drabble Botham outside the Angel Hotel in 1872 his firm had been a pioneer in the use of photography for property marketing. The widespread use of colour photographs incorporated with most agency particulars was first introduced to Chesterfield by Bothams.

During the mid 1980s the late Jack Shemwell spent many hours developing a tailor made computer system which offered a particularly effective property mailing list system and comprehensive property database. That system has since been updated and expanded with the installation of new hardware and software programs at the end of 1998 specifically developed to meet the needs of a modern estate agency.

Meanwhile in 1987 at Mitchell and Slaney, Mark Allen, another locally born Chartered Surveyor, was taken into partnership. Mark concentrated on professional survey and valuation services in addition to the established and continuing property management business.

Above: *William Colledge Botham.* ***Below:*** *Bothams worked with another auctioneer to run the Chesterfield Fat Stock Show in the 1930s.*

Following Bill Slaney's untimely death in 1991 Mark Allen continued in practice as sole principal until he employed, and subsequently took into partnership, another local Chartered Surveyor, David Tate.

With the retirement of both John and Derek Botham, direct descendants of William Drabble Botham, the continuous family link came to an end. The remaining partners however remained keen to carry the strong traditions of a family firm into the 21st century when in November 2000 the two firms merged under the name Bothams Mitchell Slaney.

The present partners Alan Terry, Mark Allen, Peter Bagnall, Mike Hinch and David Tate are all locally born and bred, experienced Chartered Surveyors who between them are able to offer unrivalled knowledge and experience. The merger of the two firms combined the strengths of Bothams in residential and commercial property sales and professional valuation markets, with Mitchell & Slaney's specialisation in property management

and continues to have one of the largest property portfolios in the area under its management.

In an age where new businesses spring up daily along our high streets Bothams Mitchell Slaney is justifiably proud of its reputation built up since the reign of Queen Victoria. The firm continues to keenly uphold traditional values whilst offering modern thinking, unrivalled local knowledge and professional experience combined with total professional independence.

__Left:__ JK Botham and WD Botham who have retired from the firm. __Below (both pictures):__ The five partners of Bothams. Top picture, David Tate and Mark Allen.

Bottom picture; from left to right; Mike T Hinch, Peter Bagnall and Alan J Terry. __Bottom:__ The modern premises in West Bars House.

Keeping the show on the road

The Bakewell Show ran smoothly in the summer of 2000 thanks to Clay Cross civil engineers, Tomlinson and White (Contracts) Ltd, who had laid tarmac on the roads within the showground. The Company was established as a partnership in 1946 by Harry White and George Tomlinson and became a Limited Company in 1961 under the management of Harry White and Ralph Brailsford as Directors.

The original business activity was as Public Works Contractors and both partners worked on-site. It is not known where the business began; however, from 1961 until 1967 Harry White's home was used and the Pig O' Lead Farm, Stone Edge, Ashover with the company's vehicles parked outside. In the early days the only machinery was a JCB Mark One Excavator which was basically a large Fordson tractor with bolt on hydraulics. Rocks in trenches were hand broken and pipes were joined with tarred gaskin and cement mortar. Today, there is a wide variety of hydraulic equipment available, making life a lot easier.

Mr Brailsford's brother, Jim, joined the Company in 1964 and Ralph, currently Managing Director, is now the only Brailsford at the Company since Jim retired to work on an environmental project. Ralph himself is planning to retire after 39 years with the business and "too much paperwork".

Originally, Harry did the office administration and Ralph did the estimating and site work; Jim worked on-site, established new contacts and worked to increase business. In the late 1960s Harry White retired and the company acquired his assets and subsequently diversified into many related activities including tarmac and concrete resurfacing, sewer construction, the sealing of disused mineshafts and recently carried out reclamation work at Cromford Mill in Derbyshire, restoring the historic site to it's former glory. Following the Markham Colliery disaster, Tomlinson and White were brought in to repair the shaft head gear and the winder house.

The firm moved premises in 1967 when they bought the old Renning Shell/BP depot from the Clay Cross Company Limited. More recently, a further move in 1989 was made to their current location at Smithy Avenue, Clay Cross.

Today, Tomlinson and White's main UK markets are Local Authorities, Developers, Consultants, The Coal Authority (formerly the National Coal Board), maintenance works for local industries and selected larger contractors and builders. The company is a Civil Engineering Contractor covering roadworks, sewers, surfacing, concrete work and foundations. With healthy order books Tomlinson & White (Contracts) Ltd look set to continue making inroads well into the new millennium.

Above: The original head office at Bridge Street, Clay Cross in 1968. **Left:** *The ex-Kenning Shell-Mex/BP depot on Bridge Street.* **Right:** *Roy Hibbard, David Hays and Ralph Brailsford.* **Below:** *The current premises pictured in 1990.*

The families of Carlisle Street, Sheepridge, celebrate the coronation of King George VI in 1936.

Acknowledgments

Thanks are due to the following people and organisations

for helping make this book possible:

G.W. Martin

Derbyshire County Council Libraries and Heritage Department

Ann Krawszik, Local Studies Librarian, Chesterfield Library

The late R Wilsher ARPS, J Hardy, H Turner, V Young, J Bond

Thanks are also due to
Margaret Wakefield who penned the editorial text and
Steve Ainsworth for his copywriting skills